FOLK*of*LORE
NORTHUMBRIA

FOLKL*of*ORE
NORTHUMBRIA

FRAN & GEOFF DOEL

For Tom, Lilian and Andrew

First published 2009

The History Press
The Mill, Brimscombe Port
Stroud, Gloucestershire, GL5 2QG
www.thehistorypress.co.uk

Reprinted 2016

British Library Cataloguing in Publication Data.
A catalogue record for this book is available from the British Library.

ISBN 978 0 7524 4890 9

Typesetting and origination by The History Press
Printed in Great Britain

CONTENTS

ACKNOWLEDGEMENTS

The authors would like to thank their editors, Matilda Richards and Beth Amphlett, at The History Press; the Tonbridge Library staff for ordering vital books; Denyse Straker, University of Kent librarian at Tonbridge, for obtaining an essential article; Rennie Weatherhead, the expert on St Ebba; Julia Carter; Robert Cronin, for the loan of books and helpful information; Philip Tait, for help on Bede and early Christianity; the Vaughn William Memorial Library of the English Folk Dance & Song Society and its librarian Malcolm Taylor, for helpful material over the years; and Philip Harvey for many enjoyable boat trips to the Farne Islands with excellent commentaries.

INTRODUCTION

The counties of Northumberland and Durham have so much in common in their religious, political and cultural history that it seems sensible for a folklore study to combine the two, especially since Northumbria was an Anglo-Saxon kingdom (albeit originally comprised of two kingdoms; Bernicia and Deira), and a dukedom into the period of the Norman Conquest. Edwin's seventh-century kingdom extended even further – southwards to York, northwards to Edinburgh and westwards into Cumbria, but we have generally resisted the temptation to follow in his footsteps because it would intrude into other distinctive rich regions of folklore, though in the cases of early saints and border ballads, a wider geographical locale would make sense.

Geographically, Northumbria has an eastern coastline of a hundred miles of windswept white beaches, low cliffs, offshore islands and rocky outcrops, with castles and ancient, beautifully situated, religious sites. Northwards the broad Tweed and the dramatic wild uplands of the Cheviots form a fifty-mile barrier to Scotland, crossed by only a few roads. Westwards the Pennines form an effective demarcation from Cumbria. Prior to the coming of the Romans, this was the land of the Brigantes, herdsmen, whose tutelary goddess Brigantia protected the fertility of her land and people. Roman occupation and the establishment of Hadrian's Wall brought a diversity of peoples along with their gods and goddesses (both Roman and from the homelands of the auxiliary troops), evidences for the worship of which survive in excavated temples and artefacts in the museums of the Wall forts; the cult of the emperor and the 'soldiers' religion', Mithraism, are well represented.

The Anglo-Saxon kings claimed descent from Woden and briefly introduced Germanic paganism into the area; the Venerable Bede gives glimpses of the seasonal aspects of this paganism which merged with Christianity to initiate a calendar of folk customs and beliefs. The pagan names for the months recorded by Bede in his *De Temporum Ratione* include 'Solmonath' (month of cakes) for February and 'Blodmonath' (month of sacrifices) for November.

Edwin (*c.* 586-633) and his successor Oswald (*c.* 604-642) both aided the Christian conversion of Northumbria, the former by a Roman mission via Canterbury and the latter (more effectively) by an Irish mission from Iona, led by St Aidan who settled on Lindisfarne. Scholars and ascetics and illuminated Bibles from Monkwearmouth,

Jarrow and Lindisfarne flourished, but this 'Golden Age of Northumbria' was shattered by Viking marauders.

The Norman Conquest of 1066 ushered in a wealth of spectacular religious architecture and a diversity of monastic life, including the re-founding of Lindisfarne, Tynemouth and Jarrow; visible remains of hermit and anchorite cells can be seen at Warkworth, Chester-le-Street and Finchale. The Northumbrian region was protected by the Prince Bishops of Durham who ruled like kings, living in Durham Castle and Bishop Auckland Palace and had their own coinage and army.

Border disputes and Anglo-Scottish warfare ended with a shared monarch in 1603. The late eighteenth and early nineteenth centuries brought great changes – the industrialisation of Tyneside and an intensive exploitation of the Northumberland-Durham coalfields along with the creation of hundreds of pit villages and their generations of miners. This way of life was, however, ruthlessly swept away in the 1980s.

Written accounts of traditions and collections of songs are more abundant here for the eighteenth and early nineteenth centuries than in other regions. William Hutchinson started the trend with books on Northumberland in 1778 and Durham in 1785, followed by Stephen Oliver's *Rambles in Northumberland* (1835), M.A. Richardson's *The Local Historian's Table Book* (1842–5) and William Henderson's *Notes on the Folk-Lore of the Northern Counties of England and the Borders* (1866). The series known as the *Denham Tracts* were printed between 1846 and 1859 and covered both counties, and the newly-founded Folk-Lore Society arranged the printing of these tracts in a scholarly edition by Dr James Hardy in 1895 and the publication of a volume on *Northumbria* by M.C. Balfour in the County Folklore series in 1903. Robert Surtees was the county historian of Durham and his massive *History and Antiquities of the County Palatinate of Durham* was published between 1816 and 1840. Shortly afterwards the Surtees Society was founded and published historical works on the area. William Brockie published his *Legends and Superstitions of the County of Durham* in 1886. The great ballad and song collections will be discussed in chapter twelve. The late Victorian and Edwardian periods were rich times for the collections of customs and songs, much being found in the nick of time before the agents of social and community dislocation got fully underway.

Fran lived for many years in Northumberland and is familiar with its folksongs. We have returned two or three times a year over the past thirty years to run summer schools and explore this fascinating and unique region

Fran and Geoff Doel, 2009

ONE

THE LAND OF DRAGONS

Dragon legends are a distinctive feature of Northumbrian folklore. The stories often use an Anglo-Saxon word for dragon, 'worm' (*wyrm*). This, along with similar features in the Northumbrian dragon stories and the epic *Beowulf* and the Scandinavian legends of dragon slayers, makes it highly likely that the Northumbrian dragon lore is Anglian and/or Scandinavian in origin.

The seventh-century Anglian church at Escomb has a splendid carved dragon on its sundial and an Anglian dragon strap-end was found at Bamburgh Castle.

In dragon lore, the dragon quellers are high caste and, as with Beowulf himself, see it as a responsibility of their position to free their societies from such menace. Or, as in the case of Wiglaf, killing the dragon befits them for the responsibility of kingship. Here we see the original mythical patterns merging into the symbolism of social responsibility, though still with a sense of the divine nature of kingship. Eventually the pattern becomes feudal, with aristocrats holding land because of an ancestor's valour in killing a dragon, or other dangerous beast such as a boar. But the stories were of course retrospective, explaining how families obtained exclusive rights in the dim and distant past.

The Laidley Worm

Francis Child in his *The English and Scottish Popular Ballads* provides several Icelandic and Danish analogues to the Bamburgh legend of 'The Laidley Worm of Spindleston Heughs'. There is also a Scottish ballad, 'Kemp Owyne' or 'Kempion', collected by Motherwell and Sir Walter Scott in their ballad collections which features an historical Knight of the Round Table, Owain, son of the Uriens, whom almost drove out the Anglian invaders from Bernicia in the sixth century. Child records a ballad entitled 'The Laidley Worm of Spindleston Heughs', originally printed in 1776, which was supplied by the Revd Lamb of Norham. The 'preamble' says it is, 'A song 500 years old, made by the old Mountain Bard, Duncan Frasier, living on Cheviot, AD 1270'. This is printed at Appendix 1.

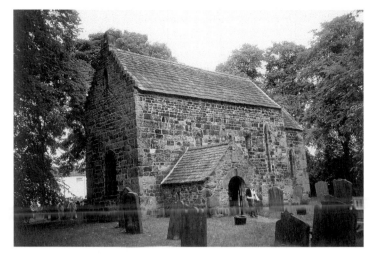

Escomb Church. (Photo: Geoff Doel)

The sundial with the dragon/ serpent, Escomb Church. (Photo: Geoff Doel)

The Spindle Stone, lair of the Laidley Worm. (Photo: Geoff Doel)

Essentially 'The Laidley Worm' is a transformation tale. A wicked and jealous stepmother transforms the daughter of the King of Bamburgh into a dragon, which curls itself around the Spindlestone, a natural feature a mile from the castle overlooking Budle Bay. The princess's brother, Child Wynd, returns and saves her, defeating magical attempts to stop him landing by the queen and her 'witch-wives'. The stepmother queen is then transformed into a venomous toad, still to be seen in the castle dungeon and environs.

Westwood and Simpson (2005) consider that the Revd Lamb wrote the ballad himself, influenced by another Northern ballad 'Kempion', in which a lady is transformed into a serpent and back again. The eighteenth century saw the creation of spurious gothic ballads and much of the 'Laidley Worm' ballad appears stylistically to have been written at this time, albeit by someone versed in ballad tradition and lore. But everything points to Lamb using an existing tradition (as often the case elsewhere with spurious ballads) and some of the more archaic phrases do not derive from 'Kempion' and could be survivals from an earlier genuine ballad or romance. Professor Child comments that, 'This composition of Mr Lamb's – for nearly every line of it is his – is not only based on popular tradition, but evidently preserves some small fragments of a popular ballad'. Also the story does not sound like an eighteenth-century invention, which would have opted for a romance rather than a brother-sister relationship.

The Spindle Stone (or Brindle Rock) is an interesting natural feature near a caravan park just to the north of Bamburgh and there used to be a cave and a stone trough associated with the worm in local tradition. The Scottish collector Kinloch writes of a variant tradition concerning the enchanted stepmother:

> The tradition of the county gives another account of the endurance of her enchantment. It is said that in the form of a toad as big as a 'clockin hen' she is doomed to expiate her guilt by confinement in a cavern in Bamborough castle, in which she is to remain in her enchanted shape until some one shall have the hardihood to break the spell by penetrating the cavern, whose 'invisible' door only opens every seven years, on Christmas eve. The adventurer, after entering the cavern, must take the sword and horn of the Childe of Wane, which hang on the wall, and having unsheathed and resheathed the sword thrice, and wound three blasts on the horn, he must kiss the toad three times; upon which the enchantment will be dissolved, and the queen will recover her human form.

The Lambton Worm

The Lambton tradition is set on the banks of the River Wear just north of Durham and concerns a prominent family and an historical figure who, as a Knight of St John on Rhodes, fought against the Turks in the fifteenth century. The Durham antiquarian Cuthbert Sharpe noted, 'John Lambton, that slewe ye worme, was knight of Rhodes and lord of Lambton, after ye dethe of fower brothers'. In this case, Sir John Lambton, like Mary Shelley's *Frankenstein*, created his own monster by going fishing on a Sunday, hooking a serpent and throwing it into a well. Whilst he was abroad crusading the serpent grew to a terrifying size, coiled around Worm Hill or Penshaw Hill (the serpentine marks it supposedly made can still be seen) and demanded a tribute of cows, sheep and milk and (in some versions) children.

Lambton Castle – the heir of the castle killed the legendary Lambton Worm.

The *Denham Tracts* quote two verses on the Worm's eating habits from a local ballad:

To the milky fold it would crawl at eve,
And at the morning's break;
And feed on the milk that nine kine gave,
In mien both soft and sleek.

But should that boon e'er be denied,
Both men and beast must fly,
Its hideous form would swell with pride,
And ire flash from its eye.

Sir John Lambton returned home to slay the worm and a witch advised him to fight in the Wear wearing a suit of armour with spikes on. The dragon coiled round Sir John, tearing itself to pieces on the spikes and the swiftly flowing Wear prevented the parts from re-uniting.

The deal done with the witch was that Sir John would kill the first living thing he met afterwards, intended to be his greyhound, but his father greeted him first. Sir John would not kill his father, so the family was cursed by seven (or nine) generations of males dying violently. Interestingly, the earliest reference to the curse is well before the full span of the generations and a remarkable number of Lambtons did meet violent ends. Sir John's son Robert was drowned and Sir William Lambton died at Marston Moor and his son William was mortally wounded fighting for the Royalists in the Civil War. The curse is supposed to have ended with the death of Henry Lambton, MP, in his carriage crossing the new bridge at Lambton in 1761. There was certainly much speculation about the curse locally in the eighteenth century.

Worm Hill is 50ft high on the north bank of the river, though later versions of the legend say the dragon preferred to coil around Penshaw Hill; Worm Well has been

A nineteenth-century engraving of
the Lambton Worm.

restored. The old Lambton mansion, Sir John's sword, the trough from which the dragon
drank and portions of the dragon's skin examined by the antiquarian Robert Surtees
have all disappeared. Two statues – of Sir John and the witch – survive on the estate.
The famous folk song 'The Lambton Worm', still sung in folk clubs and elsewhere, was
written by C.M. Leumans in 1867 (*see* Appendix 2).

The Sockburn Worm

Further south on the River Tees there is another dragon-slaying tradition at Sockburn,
linked to the Conyers family, the tenure for land and the succession of the Bishops of
Durham. The Bowes Manuscript gives the earliest account of the dragon-slayer:

> Sir John Conyers, Knight, slew the monstrous and poisonous vermin, wyvern, asp, or
> werme, which had overthrown and devoured many people in fight; for that the scent of
> the poison was so strong that no person might abyde it. And by the providence of the
> Almighty God, the said John Conyers, Knight, overthrew the said monster and slew it
> … That place where this great serpent lay was Graystone, and this John lyeth buried in
> Sockburne Church in compleat armour of the time before the conquest.

There is a fourteenth-century effigy of an armoured knight thought to be Sir John
Conyers in the Conyers Chapel in the ruined All Saints' Church, Sockburn, with a
dragon at his feet. This chapel is famous as the site of the crowning of Highbald as
Bishop of Lindisfarne in 781 and of Eanbold as Archbishop of York in 796. The dragon
is supposed to be buried under the Graystone in a nearby field. The trough where the
Sockburn Worm drank its milk and bathed itself was still visible in Victorian times.

Each new bishop was presented with a falchion by the Lord of Sockburn Manor at a
ceremony at either Neasham Ford, or on Croft Bridge if the river was in flood, the most

The Conyers Falchion, used to kill the Sockburn Dragon. (Courtesy of the Treasury, Durham Cathedral)

southerly entrances to the County Palatine. The owner of Sockburn Manor referred to the bishop as 'Count Palatine' and 'Earl of Sandberge' and made the following speech:

> My Lord Bishop, I here present you with the falchion wherewith the champion Conyers slew the worm, dragon, or fiery flying serpent, which destroyed man, woman and child; in memory of which the king then reigning gave him the manor of Sockburn, to hold by this tenure, that upon the first entrance of every bishop into this county this falchion should be presented.

The bishop then took the falchion into his hand, and, immediately returning it, wished the Lord of Sockburn health and a long enjoyment of the manor.

Hugh Pudsey purchased the title of the Earl of Sandberge for himself and his successors from Richard the Lionheart and it is thought that the ceremony originated at this time. The Conyers family claimed to be Saxon landowners and were hereditary constables of Durham in Norman times; they certainly held the tenure of the land of the banks of the Tees by 1396, and one document claims they owned it from the eleventh century. Their house no longer survives and the Conyers direct line ended in the nineteenth century, their estates being taken over by the Blacketts of Newcastle-upon-Tyne. The Mayor of Darlington now makes the presentation. The falchion used to be kept at Sockburn Hall, but is now in the Treasury of Durham Cathedral. It is of thirteenth-century workmanship with what is claimed (unhistorically) to be the arms of Morcar, Anglo-Saxon earl of the area, a black eagle on a gold field on one side and the three Plantagenet lions in gold against a red enamelled field on the reverse. The blade is steel, with a bronze guard decorated with winged biting serpents with interlaced bodies and tails, and a pommel with a wooden grip.

Over 1,000 gentry often attended the ceremony. Bishop Cosin describes his reception of the falchion in 1661:

The confluence and alacritie of the gentry, clergy, and other people, was very great, and on my first entrance through the River Tease, there was scarce any water to be seene for the multitude of horses and men that filled it, when the sword that killed the dragone was delivered to me with all the formality of trumpets, and gunshots, and acclamations that might be made.

The Longwitton Dragon

There are three wells in the grounds of Longwitton Hall, near Rothbury, which were famed for their curative powers. Everyone had recourse to them and they were the scene of a Midsummer festival, when people drank the waters.

According to legend, a dragon took possession of the wells, and was discovered by a ploughman; 'It had coiled its tail round one of the trees and pushed its long black tongue into the wall and was lapping the water like a dog.'

The dragon became invisible and no one could now approach the wells because they could feel the heat from the dragon's breath, or see its footprints or evidence of its movements. The dragon created a whirlwind to prevent the villagers from attacking it. Eventually a passing knight (in some versions Guy of Warwick) took on the dragon, but the dragon's wounds healed quickly due to the curative properties of the wells. After three combats the knight realised that the dragon always fought with its tail in a well. On his fourth attack the knight pretended to be wounded and as the dragon moved in for the kill, ensured he was between the dragon and the well. He resumed the fight and without the healing waters the dragon became enfeebled and died.

The Drake or Dragon's Stone, Harbottle, Northumberland is a dramatic rock formation 30ft high, rising above Harbottle Crag in Coquetdale. It was believed to possess healing properties and sick children were passed over it to be cured as late as the nineteenth century.

Wild Boars

The Pollard Boar tradition in Bishop Auckland shares features with dragon legends as a test of bravery resulting in an award of lands. An enormous wild boar terrorised the bishop's land and the bishop offered a reward for its capture. A local young man, Pollard, observed that the boar's favourite food was beechnuts. He shook down the nuts, which the boar ate and after gorging itself, it fell asleep. Pollard attacked the boar with a spear and a fierce fight ensued, which lasted through the night. Pollard was victorious, but was so exhausted that all he could do was cut out the boar's tongue and fall asleep. On awaking he found that someone had cut off and taken away the boar's head. He rode to the bishop's palace, where a stranger was presenting the beast's head to the prelate and claiming the prize. Fortunately Pollard could produce the tongue as proof of his victory and was rewarded by riding round and staking his land while the bishop dined. Pollard encircled the castle, but the bishop offered him a large stretch of fertile land 'with pastures, and meadows, and woodland' instead, which the people of Bishop Auckland have called Pollard's Lands ever since.

Brancepeth Castle – said to be the haunt of a giant boar. (From the *Monthly Chronicle* 'North-Country Lore and Legend', 1890)

The Callaly Boar, Callaly Castle

The Lord of Callaly planned his new castle to be built on a hill, though his wife desired it to be in the valley at Shepherd's Shaw where the site was sheltered. The castle walls were built on the hill under the direction of the master builder, but the next day they were found pulled down and scattered over the hillside. After this had happened several times the master builder kept watch at night and saw a massive boar standing on its hind legs, using its front legs like great arms to tear down the castle wall, after which it cried out:

Callaly Castle built on a height
Up in the day, down in the night,
Build it down in the Shepherd's Shaw, ★
It will stand for ever and never fa'.

Callaly castle stands on a height;
It's up in the day and down at night;
Set it up on the Shepherd's Shaw,
There it will stand and never fa'.

★Alternative '*Build it in a bog, / And it will neither shake nor shog*'.

The Brawn of Brancepeth

The Brawn of Brancepeth is said to be twelfth century; it made its lair on Brandon Hill and was killed by Roger de Ferry.

TWO

FAERIE FOLK

The Revd John Horsley, in his *Materials for the History of Northumberland*, gathered in 1729–30, claims that fairy stories in his day 'seem now to be much worn both out of date and out of credit', but Denham argues against this. According to the *Denham Tracts*:

> The not yet exploded belief in the Fairies connects itself with Fairy Slippers, Fairy Stones, Fairy Butter, Fairy Pipes … Fairy Cups, Fairy Cauldrons, Fairy Wells, Fairy Hills, Fairy Rings, Fairy Money, Elf Locks, Elf Shots, Fairy Cakes, Fairy Javelins, Fairy Kettles, Fairy Loaves, Fairy Mushrooms, Elf Arrows, Puck Fists, Fairy Flax, Fairy Bells [i.e. the flower of the Foxglove], Fairy Fingers, Fairy or Colpixy Heads, Elf Fire, Elf Knots, Fairy Saddles etc.

The faerie or fairy genus included the 'little' (or 'good') people as well as brownies, elves, goblins, sprites, pixies and bogles and all the names of the latter were once well known in the North: Bluecap, Dunnie, Dobie, Brown Man of the Moor, Redcap, Headless Hob, Hobthrush, Cauld Lad of Hilton, Pelton Brag, Picktree Brag and Hedley Kow etc.

The 'little people' looked and dressed like scaled-down humans and often had wings; they lived in rounded hills or ancient burial mounds, but though 'fair of face and form' they were very far from being harmless and men did well to avoid them. Hodgson, in his *History of Northumberland*, claimed that:

> A number of then dwelt apart in the remotest glen of … the Cheviot Hills, where among a most desolate scene of plashy bogs, and dashing waterfalls, up among grey craggy declivities, and slopes of treacherous and slippery boulders, is the opening of a cavern … In this gloomy receptacle they are said to have once lured a party of hunters who were in pursuit of a roe.

Other fairy locations identified by nineteenth-century collectors include: Fawdon Hill, reputed site of a fairy court; the banks of Fosterland Burn, where sweet fairy music was reportedly heard by an old thresher; the Dancing Green at Debdon near Rothbury; and the Dancing Green Knowe in the Cockenheugh range of hills. Dancing is of course what fairy people do on a moonlit night and the inhabitants of Chillingham regularly saw fairies dancing round the Hurle Stane 'to the sound of elfin music'. It was claimed that Alnwick was full of fairies. Tate tells us:

There was a Fairies' Green not far from Vittry's Cross; but on moonlight nights these tiny folk dropped out of dell, and cavern, and mine, and from beneath the bracken, and from under green knows, and out of other lonely places, to hold their revels with music and dance in the Fairies' Hollow at the top of Clayport Bank.

Once, a procession of fairies was seen by a miller's boy at Rothley Mill near Cambo coming from the nearby Elf Hills. 'Dressed in green, their hair was the colour of flax. Musicians piped their way and they rode on cream-coloured fairy horses whose harnesses rang with tinkling bells.' The miller's boy tried to drive them back by throwing stones at them, but they pursued him as he ran back to the mill and 'punished him with a blow in the back which caused him to be lame for life'.

Signs of a (generally unseen) fairy population were everywhere in the North. The ruins of an extensive building with hypocausts (part of the Roman station of Chesterholm), was popularly known as a 'fairy kitchen'. Some old field pastures on Tweedside, North Durham, had ridges cast up by the plough known as 'elf-furrows'. Beaumont Water, on the north of Cheviot, has a gravelly bed with small stones 'of a rounded or spiral form,' locally known as 'fairy cups' and 'fairy dishes'. To the north of the village of Gunnerton, in Northumberland, a small burn runs in a rocky channel 'with many curious perforations', known by the country people as 'fairy kerns'. The white-flowered *linum catharticum* or purging flax, which grows in natural pastures, is called by shepherds in Berwickshire 'fairy lint' and was believed to provide fairy women with 'materials for their distaff'. And according to the *Table Book*, in the grounds of Brinkburn Priory is a fairy cemetery where the 'last of the [Northumbrian] fairy race' are interred in a shady green spot 'among the foxglove, woodruff, figwort and other flowers they loved.'

A description of the fairy court at Fawdon Hill appears in a story collected by the *Monthly Chronicle* for the year 1891:

A farmer, riding past Fawdon Hill at midnight, was surprised to hear the sound of music and jollity in so lonely a place. On coming nearer, he became aware of a door open in the hillside, and through it saw strange-looking dwarfed people seated at a banquet. One of the attendants, perceiving the stranger, offered him a cup full of liquor, which he accepted; but, instead of drinking the contents to his entertainers' health, he prudently spilt them on the ground, and putting spurs to his horse, fled incontinently. The swiftness of the beast enabled him to baffle his pursuers, so that he bore away the empty vessel which was afterwards found to be made of some unknown substance. This is a very old story, first told by a monkish chronicler, named William of Newbury, who died in 1208.

The danger of fairies lay in their predilection for human children. At Chathill Farm, north of Alnwick there was a famous 'fairy ring'. It was believed that children could dance around the ring any number of times so long as it was less than nine; any child who exceeded the prescribed number of rounds fell immediately into the fairies' power and later disappeared, never to be seen again. A nineteenth-century tale was told in Alnwick of a trap that fairies laid for children: '[it] was customary there for the fairies to lay [out] "goodies" and presents of food for cleanly children, but when the parents became aware of it the practice was discontinued.' A watchful parent utilised an old protective charm – 'the root and seedes [of peony], hanged about the necke of children, is good against … the haunting of the fairies and goblins.' Other effective charms included a piece of rowan or a four- or five-leafed clover.

There was a deep quarry near Middridge which was said to be the haunt of fairy folk. Local tradition claimed that no one would be able to ride his horse nine times round the quarry without raising the wrath of the fairy folk. One village boy did it – but took the precaution of filling his pockets with tiny pieces of rowan bark. On his ninth circuit an irate fairy appeared and pursued the boy on foot; he was as fast as the horse and brandished a fairy javelin in his hand. The boy galloped for his life, strewing the rowan bark behind him. He managed to reach the stable, and slammed and barred the door behind him just as the javelin embedded itself in the doorpost.

Whereas peony root and rowan always proved effective, a four- and five-leafed clover occasionally had an unfortunate side effect – it made the invisible visible:

> Many years ago a girl who lived near Netherwitton, returning home from milking with a pail upon her head, saw many fairies gambolling in the fields, but which were invisible to her companions, though pointed out to them by her. On reaching home and telling what she had seen of her power of vision being greater than that of her companions was canvassed in the family, and at length discovered in the 'wise' (a circular pad made of old stocking or wreath of straw or grass to save the head from the pressure of the pail) … [a] four leafed clover.

The girl was fortunate that her new abilities had not been spied by the fairies, for they would have had her removed from the earth. The following traditional story from Durham shows us that local wise women could be applied to for advice regarding protection against the fairies.

There were once fairies living in caves near Stanhope in Weardale. Because they had been observed by a farmer's child they determined to steal her away as a punishment. The girl's father consulted a wise woman who informed him that when the fairy horde arrived in the house the fairies' power would be as naught only if there was unbroken silence in the house. The farmer arranged that all his farm beasts should be silent when they arrived but had forgotten his daughter's little spaniel; its barking broke the spell and the girl was spirited away.

Fairies were feared for their propensity to steal babies in the cradle. The real baby was whisked away and never seen again, whilst a simulation of the baby (often a male adult fairy) was left to be fed and cared for by a human mother and father. These were the Changelings; they often appeared stupid or deformed. One tale states that, a woman had a child that was remarkably puny. It was voracious enough 'but put all the meat it got within an ill skin,' and never grew any, and there were shrewd suspicions that it was a changeling. One day a neighbour came running into her house and shouted out, 'Come here, and ye'll see a sight! Yonder's the Fairy Hill a' alowe. 'Waes me! What'll come o' my wife and bairns?' screamed out the elf in the bed, and straightway made its exit up the chimney.

Sometimes a fairy would shape-change into a domestic cat in order to be fed and kept warm by a human family. There are many variants of this particular tale:

A Staindrop farmer was crossing a bridge at night when a big grey cat jumped out in front of him and said, 'Tell Madam Mumfort that Mally Dixon's deed'. The farmer got home and related this to his wife whereupon Madam Mumfort their old black cat jumped up and to their astonishment said, 'Is she? Then aa mun off,' and bolted out the door.

Penshaw Hill where there was said to be a fairy community. (From the *Monthly Chronicle* – 'North-Country Lore and Legends', 1898)

Fairy folk lived and moved amongst humans unseen, but the application of a magic fairy ointment to the eyes made them visible to humans. A fairy couple once left their child with a childless shepherd and his wife in Netherwitton. He received it along with a box of ointment, with which he was enjoined regularly to rub the child's eyes, but was warned not to touch his own with it, as this would 'incur a heavy penalty'. Overcome by curiosity, he anointed one of his eyes. At first he saw nothing untoward, but, having gone to Long Horsley fair, he saw the fairy man and woman moving about the fair people, and thinking there could be no harm in it he accosted them. Surprised to be thus recognised, they enquired with what eye he saw them, and he told them, whereupon they took revenge by plucking out the man's eye and removing the child.

Stories about 'fairy butter' are plentiful in the North. Mr Denham in a letter relates:

> A story is told here [Pierse Bridge] of some women going into the field to work rather earlier one morning than usual … and found as much as nearly a pound [of fairy butter] upon the top of a gate post, how they carefully gathered it into a basin, and how they each and all partook, and found it to be 'the nicest butther that ony o' them had iver taisted.'

'Fairy butter' is the poisonous fungus *trenmella mesenterica* (yellow brain fungus). It thrives on rotted wood and is reputed to look like small pats of yellow butter.

Accepting and eating any kind of fairy food put one into the power of the fairies, but refusing fairy food was equally dangerous as it was said that the fairies did not appreciate their gifts being rejected. The following story of Penshaw Hill was once well known and concerns a colony of fairies that lived on the slopes and patted their butter in the dark.

Once, a man was passing by Penshaw Hill at night when he heard the noise of fairies patting butter and he heard a voice say, 'Mend that peel!' He passed by the next day at the same time and this time found a broken peel (a flat wooden bread shovel) lying on the ground. So he took it up and mended it. The day after that when going along the road with his cart, there was a piece of freshly baked bread set out on a stone under a hedge, spread with delicious fresh-churned butter. The man knew better than to eat it, and he did he want to give it to his horses. The upshot was, that before he got to the top of the 'lonnin' (the path running by the side of the road) both his horses fell down dead. 'And thus was he condignly punished for his want of faith in the fairies' honour.'

Fairy hills have great treasure hidden within them, but the little people see no reason to benefit humans without demanding recompense and if their domain is invaded or threatened they always use powerful magic to guard or hide their hoard. Bamburgh Castle, standing on a massive rocky outcrop, is said to have fairy money hidden in a crevice. Anyone who is naturally lucky can find the hoard. Those who find the bounty may carry it away every time they visit the place, but in return must leave one silver coin in the cleft which will be retrieved by the fairy people. If the payment is not given the fairies will withdraw the treasure completely.

Castle Hill, a twelfth-century motte near Bishopton village, was once held to be a fairy hill and was also associated with fairy treasure. At one point it was decided to level it to the ground, but just as the work began a mysterious disembodied voice was heard asking 'Is all well?'

'Yes,' was the reply.

'Then keep well when you are well,' rejoined the voice, 'and leave the Fairy Hill alone.'

The warning was not heeded and the levelling continued only to come to a halt as the workmen came across a great black oak treasure chest; so heavy was it that several men were needed to dig it out and carry it to the village blacksmith's shop 'hoping to find it full of gold or silver'. It was broken open, but 'alas, it turned out to be full of nails.'

Bamburgh Castle. (From Sir Walter Scott's *Marmion*, 1855 edition)

The Ugly Fairies

Traditionally Fairy Folk are usually exquisitely formed and of beautiful aspect and live in courtly communities. But there are other types of fairies, the bogles, goblins, and brownies etc who are of a solitary disposition and appear as ugly older men of stunted growth. Many are linked to a particular pit, farm or village and never leave the vicinity. Most display some very bad human characteristics such as a malicious sense of humour or an inexplicable desire to cause mayhem. Almost all display varying and unnerving supernatural abilities; they can shape-shift, de-materialise, assume total invisibility or take on plurality of form.

Robert Surtees, the historian of Durham, was told a story of the Brown Man by an old dame named Elizabeth Cockburn. In the year before the Great Rebellion (that of 1715) two young men from Newcastle-upon-Tyne were sporting on the high moors above Elsdon, and at last sat down to refresh themselves in a green glen near a mountain stream. After their repast, the younger lad ran to the brook for water, and after stopping to drink, was surprised, on lifting his head again, by the appearance of a brown dwarf, who stood on a crag covered with bracken across the burn. This remarkable personage did not appear to be above half the statue of an ordinary man, but was uncommonly stout and broadly built, having the appearance of vast strength; his dress was entirely brown, the colour of the bracken, and his head covered with frizzled red hair; his countenance was expressive of the most savage ferocity, and his eyes glared like those of a bull.

Addressing the awestruck young man, he threatened vengeance for having trespassed on his demesnes, asking him if he knew in whose presence he stood. The youth replied that he supposed him to be the lord of the moors, but added that he had offended through ignorance, and offered to bring him the game he had killed. This seemed to mollify the dwarf a little; nevertheless, he protested that nothing could be more offensive to him than such an offer. For, he said, 'I consider the wild animals as my subjects and never fail to avenge their destruction. I do not feed on anything that has life. In the summer I subsist on whortle-berries, cloud-berries, dew-berries and craneberries, with nuts and mushrooms for a change; and in winter my food is hazel nuts and crab apples, wild plums and sloes, of which I have great store in the woods.'

The strange figure then invited the youth to partake of his hospitality. The lad was about to accept the invitation when he heard the call of his companion. Turning to tell him that he would be with him soon, he was surprised to find, on looking round again, that the wee man had fled. Elizabeth Cockburn's information was that the youth paid so little heed to the warning he had got from the Brown Man that he continued his day's sport across the moors.

The Hazelrigg Dunnie was a mischievous brownie that plagued cottagers and farmhands who lived on and near Belford Moor. Its usual prank was to enter into cottages during the night and up-end the furniture. Another of its tricks was to assume the likeness of a plough-horse and stand quietly until it was yoked whereupon it would evaporate while screaming with laughter. The *Denham Tracts* believed that the dunnie had once been mortal and a reputed reiver who hoarded his gear and ill gotten gains in the moorlands and crags. It took the concerted efforts of all the farmhands on the two Hazelrigg farms to kill him when he was caught stealing corn. As a brownie, he liaised with the fairies in substituting changeling children in farmhouses and cottages. Like the kow (see below), he was particularly fond of causing mischief when midwives were sent for, often shape-shifting into the horse which brought the midwife to the mother-to-be. He would gallop over the moor carrying the midwife and the serving lad who had been sent to get her and just as they reached the door of the cottage where she was needed, he would rear up and tip them both into a muck heap or mire.

Locals often spotted the dunnie in a quarry for he took an airing at night and used to sit on the steepest part of the cliff and dangle his legs. One tradition according to the *Denham Tracts* claims that he can be heard sadly lamenting the great treasure he once buried on moorland tracts and on the crags.

There was another species of brownie in northern England known variously as the hob, or as hobthrusts and hobthrushes. They were typically described as small in stature, bulky in build, incredibly hairy and with a tail. One incredibly industrious and helpful hobthrush used to visit Elsdon village and did household chores and handy work until the housewives, thinking to reward him, clubbed together and bought him a new hat to replace his old threadbare one, completely unaware that this was how communities traditionally rid themselves of unwelcome spirits. Poor hobthrush exited into the stratosphere with a banshee-like wail and the ladies, having lost their home help, were understandably disconsolate.

Another brownie, called Headless Hob or Hob Hedeless – presumably he had lost his head – regularly roamed the road between Naworth and Neasham until he was entrapped by a spell and imprisoned under a huge boulder by the roadside; the punishment was intended to last 'for ninety-nine years and a day'. It was claimed that anyone sitting on the stone would be glued to it forever. The stone was later used for building materials when a new road was constructed.

The tiny tidal island off Lindisfarne used by St Cuthbert is called Hob Thrush Island and the saint is said to have exorcised the resident hobthrush there before constructing his hermitage.

Imps and elves often made their homes down the pit. 'If there were knockings heard in the pit … it was a spiteful elf called Cutty Soams.' He was mischievous, but his special business and delight was to cut the traces or 'soams' by which the poor little assistant putters (sometimes girls) used then to be yoked to the wooden trams underground. His haunts were the 'sooty cavernous voids in a coal mine left after the removal of the coal'. He tampered with brattices so as to 'divert or stop the air currents', he hid the men's gear, he blunted the hewer's picks, frightened the ponies and putters 'with dismal groans and growls', exhibited deceptive blue lights, and every now and then choked 'scores of men and boys with after-damp in places where no one ever suspected the deadly presence of gas to be'.

Bluecap was a much more amenable elf and was usually 'honest and hard-working'. The miners were aware of his presence if there was a light-blue flame flickering in the air, usually settling on a full coal-tub, which immediately moved towards the rolley-way. Industrious Bluecap required, and justly so, to be paid for his services, which he modestly rated as those of an ordinary putter; therefore once a fortnight, Bluecap's wages were left for him in a solitary corner of the mine. If they were a farthing below his due, the indignant Bluecap would not pocket a stiver; if they were a farthing above his due the indignant Bluecap left the surplus revenue where he found it. One investigator asked his informant, a hewer, whether if Bluecap's wages were nowadays to be left for him, he thought they would be appropriated; the man shrewdly answered, he thought they would be taken by Bluecap – or somebody else.

At Shilbottle Colliery near Alnwick there was an imp called Blue Bonnet who also expected to have payment for his day's work. In the 1890s a newspaperman asked some of the miners if they ever saw him, but no one had as they no longer believed in him.

Brags, a common Northern term for goblins, bogles or bogeys, were once commonly found in Northumberland and Durham. The Cauld Lad of Hylton is the most famous, but also well known were the Pelton, Picktree and Portobello Brags.

This is an account given by Sir Cuthbert Sharp of an apparition of the Pelton Brag taken verbatim from the deposition of an old woman of respectable appearance of about ninety years of age, living near the spot. A galloway is a species of horse of small size but great endurance, first bred in Galloway in Scotland:

I never saw the brag very distinctly, but I frequently heard it. It sometimes appeared like a calf, with a white handkerchief about its neck, and a bushy tail. It cam' also like a galloway, but more often like a coach horse and went trotting along the lonnin, afore folks, setting up a great nicker and a whinney every now and then … My brother once saw it like four men holding up a white sheet. I was then sure that some near relation was going to die, which was true. My husband once saw it in the image of a naked man without a head. I knew a man in the name of Bewick that was so frightened that he hanged himself for fear on't. Whenever the midwife was sent for, it always came up with her in the shape of a Galloway. Dr Harrison wouldn't believe in it; but he met it one night as was going home, and it maist killed him, but he never would tell what happened and didn't like to talk about it; and whenever the Brag was mentioned he sat tremblin' and shakin' by the fireside. My uncle had a white suit of clothes, and the first time he ever put them on he met the Brag, and he never had them on afterwards but he met with some misfortune: and once when he met the Brag … having been at a Christening, he was determined to get on the Brag's back; but when he cam' to the four lonnin ends, the Brag joggled him so sore that he could hardly keep his seat, and at last it threw him off in the middle of the pond, and then ran away setting up a great nicker and laugh … when my father was dying the Brag was heard coming up the lonnin like a coach and six, and it stood before the house, and the room shaked, and it gave a terrible yell when my father died and then it went claterrin' and gallopin' down the lonnin as if yeben and yerth [heaven and earth] was comin' together.

An account from the *Monthly Chronicle of Folklore* 1891 tells us that Picktree near Chester-le-Street is famous for two reasons – first, because it was the home of the heroine of the popular song 'Ailsie Marley', and secondly, because 'it was the haunt of one of those mischievous goblins [the brag] that were formerly supposed to infest almost every old inhabited place in the North Countrie'.

The Picktree Brag used to make an appearance on the old coaching road between Chester-le-Street and Birtley. Another shape-changer, he appears to have had an interest in births and deaths. Midwives claimed that he often accompanied them as they hurried to a confinement but that he left their side soon as they knocked at the door of the house where the confinement was to take place. One story tells how he visited a dying man in the form of an invisible horse and carriage. Sorrowing friends were gathered

Hylton Castle – the scene of the Cauld Lad and other legends. (Photo: Geoff Doel)

round the bed of the dying man when they heard the noise of a coach and six tearing along the road outside. The invisible vehicle screeched to a halt in front of the dying man's house and set off again the moment when the old man breathed his last. On one occasion the brag wickedly rolled behind an old woman along the road in the shape of a big round cheese. The old wife was totally disconcerted, but when she hurried, it too speeded up. When she reached the safety of her door the rolling cheese disappeared into the night air screaming horribly.

Portobello, not far from Picktree and Pelton, also had a brag. This one only ever assumed the shape of an ass but to further discompose onlookers would dissolve uttering unnerving screams or run off 'nickerin and laughin'.

The most famous brag in the region is the Cauld Lad of Hilton Castle, and the story concerning him in the *Denham Tracts* shows how a community used an age-old trick to rid itself of a spirit by offering it new clothes.

The merry pranks of the goblin had become wearisome to the servants, and they determined upon banishing him; but the Cauld Lad, having caught an inkling of their intentions, used to amuse himself in the dead of night with chanting, in a melancholy strain:

Wae's me! Wae's me!
The acorn is not yet
Grown upon the tree
That's to grow the wood
That's to make the cradle
That's to rock the bairn
That's to grow to a man

That's to lay me!
But the Cauld Lad reckoned without his host, for the domestics provided the usual means of banishment, viz., a green cloak and a hood, which they laid before the kitchen fire. At the hour of midnight, the goblin sprite stood before the smouldering embers and surveyed the garments provided for him very attentively, then tried them on, and appeared delighted with his appearance, frisking about the room, and cutting sundry somersets and gambadoes, until at length, on hearing the first crow of the cock, twitching his green mantle about him, he disappeared with the appropriate valediction of:

Here's a cloak and here's a hood,
The Cauld Lad o' Hylton will do na mair good!

A bogle or bogie called the Hedley Kow made itself visible only in the village of Hedley near Ebchester in Durham and its environs. Though it was not perceived to be evil, it was impish and ill-behaved and as a shape-shifter caused consternation whenever it manifested itself. Every time it materialised it ended up with its unnerving trademark – raucous prolonged laughter interspersed with hoots and howls.

The following are typical stories told about the kow taken from a late nineteenth-century source:

> Goody Blake was gathering sticks by roadside. She was a poor old woman and came from the little village called Hedley. The Hedley Kow was out roving. When he spotted Goody he turned himself into a great bale of straw lying in the road. The old woman knew it was not hers to take but was tempted and struggled hard to carry him back to her cottage. Just as they neared her front door the hay became so heavy that she had to put it down whereupon it disconcertingly sprouted legs and marched before her veering sharply to the right and left. It finally dissolved into loud and harsh-sounding laughter.

Two young men from the village of Newlands near Ebchester had arranged to meet their sweethearts. They saw the girls, but they had their backs to them and were walking briskly.

The girls did not stop and the boys followed behind always quickening their pace, but the girls were faster. They walked for two or three miles, the boys never catching up, until they found themselves up to their knees in mire whereupon the two girls with a coarse laugh disappeared. Realising they had been duped by the kow, the lads fled homewards – the kow screeching and laughing at their heels. In a panic in crossing the Derwent one fell into the water and the other tumbled on top of him; their cries mingling with the delighted shrieks of the kow.

Once, a farmer called Forster living near Hedley went out into his field very early one morning, caught what he thought was his grey horse and harnessed it, yoked it to the cart and jumped up ready to drive off. But he had been deceived by the kow. It slipped away from the limmers, set up a great 'nicker' and was off into the early morning light.

Another of the kow's tricks was to torment serving girls working on farms; here he would take the form of a cow, and lead the milkmaid a chase round the field before letting her lead him into the milk shed, During the milking time he would kick and 'rowt' and at the last kick over the pail of milk, slip clear of the tie, give a loud bellow and bolt off. This trick was so commonly done that his name was derived from it.

Serving girls in the great houses were also a target. He could adopt the voice of their sweetheart and called them outside. While they were searching he would be inside upsetting the cooking pot, giving the cream to the cat, unravelling their knitting or spoiling their work on the spinning wheel.

When a woman was in labour, he was always present. This was often annoying to the man who was setting off on horseback to fetch the midwife, for one of his tricks was to make the horse stand absolutely still. No spurring or whipping would make the horse budge though the rider saw nothing. Sometimes he would permit the midwife to be picked up and be brought but as they were crossing water the kow would begin to play with his cantrips causing the horse to kick and plunge in such a way so as to dismount his double load of messenger and midwife.

Sometimes when the wife was in labour and groaning the kow would press against the window and chatter. The farmer had to take out a stick and rush out at him, but many a time the stick was pulled out of his hands and turned against him.

The Simonside Hills were said to be the home of Duergar, a truly malicious race of goblins well known on the Borderlands. Tyndale's *Legends and Folklore of Northumbria*, written in 1930, describes them as 'ugly, cross-grained little beings'. They caused travellers to lose their way and led them in the dark over the dangerous 'moss-hags' (bogs) until they stumbled into the Duergar Kingdom, from which they would never return.

THREE

GHOSTS

There was not a village … that had not its own peculiar ghosts. Nay, every lone
tenement, castle, or mansion-house, which could boast of any antiquity, had … its
spectre, or its knocker. The churches, churchyard, and cross-roads, were all haunted. Every
green lane had its boulder stone on which an apparition kept watch at night … And there
was scarcely a shepherd to be met who had not seen a spirit.

Denham Tracts

The North East has numerous 'historic' ghosts; these are apparitions of men and women
whose past (often with a violent death) is either known from oral tradition or has
been recorded and whose sightings are restricted to a specific location. Also popular are
stories of 'wraiths' (spectres in the exact likeness of a person), supposed by 'the common
people' (delightfully described by one early source as 'the vulgar') to be seen before or
soon after the person's death. But until the beginning of the twentieth century, the most
frequently recorded ghost stories were those that involved 'silkies', otherwise known as
'white ladies', or (debatably) in the silky's other aspect, 'the hag'.

A crucial factor in determining whether a ghost is a silky or not is the ghost's
relationship to water, for this is a spirit that relates to springs, rivers, stagnant ponds,
wells, waterfalls or fountains. There is another element in a silky ghost story – it is very
often associated with treasure hidden in the earth.

The 'Historic' Ghosts

John Webster, the Puritan minister whose works display an almost unwholesome
pre-occupation with the grotesque and titillating, describes a ghost sighting near
Chester-le-Street in 1631 or 1632 in his *Displaying of Supposed Witchcraft* (1677). The
ghost was soon identified. She was a murder victim, a young woman of twenty-five, and
she materialised before one John Grahame, a miller at Lumley. John was working late
one winter's evening when suddenly a neighbour, Annie Walker, appeared before him.
Annie was housekeeper to her uncle John Walker, and their house was nearby. John was
dimly aware that something was wrong because Annie's hair was 'down' and dishevelled,

but he was shaken rigid when Annie bent her head before him revealing five bloody gaping wounds in her skull. John, appalled, managed to pull his wits together and asked her what she wanted. She replied:

> I am the Spirit of such a woman, who lived with Walker, and being got by child by him, he promised me to send me to a private place, where I should be well lookt to until I was brought in bed, and well again; and then I should come again, and keep his house … I was one night late sent away with one Mark Sharp, who upon a Moor slew me with a pick … and gave me these five wounds, and after threw my body into a coal-pit hard by, and hid the pick under a bank, and his shoos [*sic*] and stockings being bloody.

The apparition also told the miller that he must be the man to reveal it, or else that she must still appear and haunt him.

The spectre appeared twice more to Grahame; on the final occasion it was when he was walking in his garden on the eve of St Thomas, just before Christmas. The following morning, John sought out a magistrate and told him 'as much as he knew'. A search was made in the coal pit and Annie's body found with five wounds in the head. The pick, shoes and stockings also were discovered with blood upon them. Annie's murderer, Mark Sharp, was a 'sworn Brother' of Walker. At the trial Walker and Sharp were both found guilty and executed.

When Darlington's 'Old Workhouse' was established it inherited a resident ghost. The workhouse was founded in the eighteenth century in Lead Yard in buildings which had previously been a manor house and, before that, a bishop's palace. In the mid-Victorian period it was taken over by Darlington Union as a poorhouse. Men were accommodated in the north of the site, women in the south and a children's playground was set in the middle. The ghost, a female, was 'left over' from the old manor house. She was one-armed, a decided mischief-maker and a shape-changer. The paupers learned to identify her by the whishing sound of silk as she moved unseen along the corridors at the dead of night or in the early morning light. When an inmate was about to die or a pauper child was about to be born she would announce the news by clashing pots together in the empty kitchen and rattling the pump handle, then pull the bedclothes off the serving girls (who slept two to a bed) and tip the girls onto the floor. After this, and only for those in the infirmary, she made invisible coffee and its delicious pungent smell would waft round the sick room.

W. Hylton Dyer Longstaffe in his *History of the Parish of Darlington* (1854) identified her as an 'historic' ghost, a certain Lady Jaratt, wife of Charles Jaratt, and daughter of Dr John Cosin, Bishop of Durham. In the seventeenth century, Lady Jaratt and her husband lived in the manor house. It was believed that she had suffered a violent death, being murdered by soldiers (possibly Parliamentary troops) who had cut off one of her arms in order to retrieve the expensive rings on her fingers. For many years the bloody marks of her thumb and fingers were said to have marked the poorhouse walls, but generations of workhouse paupers with buckets of water and scrubbing brushes had ultimately eroded the stains. One of her habits as a ghost was to sit forlornly on the churchyard wall – frightening generations of children on their way to and from school.

Raby Castle. The castle is reputed to have three ghosts: Henry Vane the Younger, Sir Charles Neville and Lady Barnard. (Photo: Geoff Doel)

Raby Castle may have three 'historic' ghosts: Headless Henry Vane the Younger, Sir Charles Neville, and Lady Barnard. Headless Henry sometimes appears in the library, where he is rehearsing a speech, but Sir Charles, one of the leaders of the Northern Rebellion (1569), rarely makes an appearance. Surtees, the Durham county historian, wrote to Sir Cuthbert Sharp regarding the unnerving ghostly activities of the third ghost, Lady Barnard:

> This old jade after her death used to drive about in the air, in a black coach and six; sometimes she takes the ground and drives slowly up to town to Alice's Well, and still more frequently walks the battlements of Raby, with a pair of brass knitting needles, and is called Old Hell Cat.

Sometimes stories are so old that all the details get lost. One nineteenth-century clergyman wrote:

> No one living at Wooler knew anything of Dudley Brechan, but … the spirit of Dudley Brechan haunted the 'Big House', on the Tenter's Hill, a bulky, red-tiled, and white-washed mansion, one of a row, built on a ridge, where the dyers of Wooler were wont, in former days, to stretch their webs to dry … When the ghost paid its evening visits, its descent was like a 'meikle cupple' falling with a crash on the ceiling. Many a 'gliff' the folk got; but beyond frightening them it perpetrated no other mischief.

There are accounts of clergymen being approached to drive out unhappy spirits. Andrew Bates, curate of St John's Church, Newcastle-upon-Tyne, from 1689 to 1710, became quite famous for successfully exorcising a number of haunted houses, in particular for 'laying', as they stated it, the ghost of one Barbara Cay, wife of a Mr Cay, a Presbyterian of fortune and reputation in Newcastle-upon-Tyne, after all the Presbyterian ministers had failed.

An early rectory house at Sedgefield was burned down in 1792 and the locals were relieved because in its last years it was haunted by the ghost of an ex-parson. An explanation of why he came to be known as the 'Pickled Parson' is given in an account written in 1887:

> … a rector's wife had the ill-luck to lose her husband a week before the farmers' tithes fell due. Prompted by avarice, she cunningly concealed his death by salting the body of her departed spouse, and retaining it in a private room. Her schemes succeeded, she received the emoluments of the living, and the next day made the decease of the rector public. Since the fire, the apparition has not been seen.

Beyldon (also known as Building) Hill near Monkwearmouth not only had a ghost, it was also associated with wraiths. William Brockie, in his *Legends and Superstitions of … Durham* (1886) says, 'an intelligent middle-aged lady tells me that she remembers quite well how, when she was a young girl, the people used to go out to the hill at midnight to see the ghost'. An even earlier reference of a ghostly sighting on this hill comes from a deposition made in 1767 and states that a 'Waugh [wraith] had been observed walking abroad there. William Brockie in his *Legends* says, 'vulgar tradition has it that Mr Wesley went out himself to Beyldon Hill, and laid the Ghost', but is adamant that an entry in John Wesley's journal proves that he had gone there with five companions simply to give spiritual support and to pray while a woman called Elizabeth Hobson climbed the hill to encounter the ghost:

> We came thither a little before twelve, and then stood at a small distance from her. It being a fine night we kept her in sight, and spent the time in prayer. She stood there till a few minutes after one. When we saw her move, we went to met her. She said, 'Thank God, it is all over and done'.

Elizabeth, a visionary who constantly saw the wraiths of people about to die, identified the ghost on the hill as that of her grandfather John Hobson whom she described as 'an exceeding wicked man'.

The Carrs are grassy fields on high land to the north-east of Tanfield, five miles west of Darlington and on the south bank of the Tees. They were once the haunt of an unquiet ghost in the early part of the nineteenth century. In life the ghost had been a farmer named Stephen Hollis. He had farmed the Carrs and had been a familiar figure striding along his 'long, grey fields' in his 'brown suit and low-crowned hat'. One day he was brutally murdered by his two nephews and buried in his own fields. When his absence was investigated the murderers dug him up and burned the body in a brick oven. For many years, the presence of Stephen Hollis was recorded by locals and anything untoward was attributed to him. Strange noises on a farm would bring the retort, 'It's only Stephen'. If the door to the milking parlour would not shut, it was Stephen who was holding it open. If the horses were 'all of a lather' in their stalls in the morning, it was because Stephen had been riding them through the night. Often his low-crowned hat would be seen passing behind a hedge.

The following ghost story, 'Aad Wilson', was recorded by a collector in the late nineteenth century, but the events were said to have taken place in the 1840s:

A farmer named Wilson who had been attending Stockton market, and left that town at a late hour, rather the worse for drink, to ride home to Middlesbrough, lost his way in the dark and rode into the Tees where he was drowned. His body was recovered soon after, but his hat, as was natural, had disappeared. His ghost was said to appear, causing terror to belated travellers. A local Methodist preacher named John Orton, who had been at Middlesbrough, conducting divine service, was returning alone one night to Stockton, when, about the locality where the farmer was lost, he met a man without any hat, to whom he bade 'Good night', but received no answer. It being near midnight and the place quite solitary, Orton wondered what the man could be doing at that untimely hour. He therefore turned around and followed him, to see, if possible, where he went but after retracing a few steps, he lost sight of him all of a sudden, the man disappearing, or rather vanishing into a bush on the left-hand side of the road; when Orton went cautiously forward and peered into the bush there was no living creature there or here about. When he reached home, and told his wife what he had seen, she instantly exclaimed, 'Why, man, it's been aad Wilson!'

Stephen Oliver, the author of *Rambles in Northumberland and on the Scottish Borders* (1835), tells that in passing a remote Northumbrian cottage in the 1830s he, 'remembered an old woman who had dwelt there and who was suspected of having caused the death of one of her children'. He enquired of a native of the village if he knew anything of the circumstance, and received the following account:

I knew the woman ... she was the wife of a 'day-tale' man and they had more small bairns than they could well provide for; and in harvest she used to go out a-shearing. One year, about the harvest time, she had a young bairn at the breast, which she thought was one too many; and that she might not be hindered at the shearing by staying at home with it, and that she might get rid of it altogether, she smothered it in the cradle. There was no public enquiry made, nor inquest held, but all her neighbour, especially the women folk, believed that the bairn was wilfully made away with ... she never did well, though she lived for nearly forty years afterwards. She fell into a low way, and was at times almost clean past herself. She was always at the worst about the time of the harvest moon; and would then often walk about the house, and sometimes go out and wander about the common, all night, moaning and greeting (crying) in a painful way. I have many a time seen her holding her head atween her hands, rocking herself backwards and forwards on a low chair, groaning and sighing ... About the harvest time, she often used to see the spirit of the innocent that she had put to death; and her neighbours often heard her talking to it, bidding it to be gone, and not to torment her longer with its cries.

Silkies, White Ladies & Hags

The silky of Belsay and the Black Heddon area near Stamfordham 'haunted the greenwood, the waterfall, the lonely lanes, and the isolated'. She was called 'silky' because of the rustling of her dress, which was dark brocade. A single traveller on horseback would suddenly find that she was seated behind him, and accompany him for a while before melting into the night. Farmers knew when she was on the road because farm horses would suddenly halt and refuse to budge. They also knew how to get rid of her by carrying a branch of rowan, the mountain ash, which made them immune to her magic.

Sometimes at night she used to wander over a nearby crag 'finely studded with trees'. She must have had the strength of ten men, for the peasantry observed her 'splitting great stones' or hewing some mighty tree. Her presence was indicated by the sound of a storm whipping through the woods, 'the branches creaking in violent concussion, or rent into fragments by the impetuous fury of the blast'. At the bottom of the crag was a lake fed by a waterfall. At its top stood a 'venerable tree' and here the silky would sit in a crude seat, 'wind-rocked, enjoying the rustling of the storm … and the gush of the cascade'; it still bears the name 'Silky's Seat'.

A story is told about a poor farm hand that was sent to fetch coal from a colliery:

> It was late in the evening before he could return and silky waylaid him at a bridge … now known as 'Silky's Bridge' (just to the south of Black Heddon) on the road between that place and Stamfordham. As he reached [it] the horse froze, and both man and horses [would have continued] quaking and sweating, and stock-still … had not a neighbouring servant came up to the rescue, who opportunely carried some of the potent witchwood about his person. It was said that 'throughout her disembodied career, she can scarcely be said to have performed one benevolent action'.

A silky once appeared to a serving girl at Black Heddon; she was said to be, 'frightened to fits by the apparition of something tumbling from the ceiling of an old house'. It turned out to be gold coins wrapped in black cloth.

Denton Hall had a silky. Richardson in his *Table Talk* (1842–5) mentions it as a well-established phenomena:

> In the neighbourhood I found that the house was regularly set down as 'haunted', all the country round, and that the spirit …was familiarly known by her name of 'Silky' … I have heard … that at midnight curtains have been drawn by an arm clad in rustling silks; and the same form clad in dark brocade has been seen gliding along the dark corridors of that ancient, grey, and time-worn mansion.

The Hag Peg Powler is undoubtedly the most famous silky of the North and her domain is the River Tees, which rises in the Pennines and flows eastwards for eighty-five miles to the North Sea. The word *Teis* (Tees) is Celtic and means 'bubbling, or surging' and is an apt description of how the river looks after heavy downpours or when melting snows come down from the hills to join it, when the river 'thunders down as a barrage of water'. Peg is described as a terrifying hag, with green skin, long, dishevelled hair and sharp pointed teeth. 'Many are the [cautionary] tales still told at Piersbridge, of Peg dragging naughty children in its deep waters [and drowning them] when playing, despite the orders and threats of their parents, on its banks – especially on the Sabbath day.' Foam and froth on the Tees had the name of Peg Powler's Suds, and Peg Powler's Cream.

Blenkinsopp Castle is said to be visited by the White Lady. (From the *Monthly Chronicle* – 'North-Country Lore and Legend', 1888)

According to the *Denham Tracts*:

> ... a wood between Yeavering and Akeld ... is haunted by a 'white lady', who appears to walk there during the night to frighten people. The white lady near Whittingham, [is connected] with a well close to the River Aln above that village, situated at the Lee or Leaside ... by the name of the Lady Well or Lady's Well ... At Detchant, near Belford, is ... a 'Cattle Well,' which was frequented by a 'White Lady.' I could ascertain nothing more of her from the old man, who had heard of it in his youth. Detchant, he told me, was wont to be a lonely place, and was infamous for robberies committed near it.

The Revd Matthew Culley provided this account of a white lady that haunted Coupland Castle on the River Glen. His letter is dated 17 August 1880:

> As to who she is, wherefore she appears, or when she first appeared, tradition is silent; but it is certain that half a century ago the 'haunted room' at Coupland had as 'uncanny' a reputation as it has at present. Within my own memory, and indeed quite recently, strange phenomena have been witnessed, and many unaccountable sounds, such as wailing voices, knockings, &c., have been heard at night by persons sleeping in the haunted room and in rooms close by; whilst during the last six or seven years the White Lady herself is said to have been seen on more than one occasion.

It is claimed that a gloomy vault under Blenkinsopp Castle has hidden in it a large chest full of gold, 'some say by a lady whose spirit cannot rest so long as it is here and who formerly appeared clothed in white from head to foot'. The last sighting of the White Lady was about 1810 in an estate worker's cottage, when she materialised before a child in bed, kissed him and begged him to go with her as she had great wealth buried in the vault and would make him rich. She tried to carry him away forcibly, but he cried out and she vanished just as his parents entered the room. This happened three times, then they moved him to another bedroom and he did not see her again. The collector of the story adds with relish, 'Over thirty years later the "child" insisted that the story was true and would shudder when he remembered the event as if he still felt her cold lips press his cheek and her warm arms in death-like embrace'.

Meg of Meldon was a silky cum white lady cum hag figure. A famed spectre and reputed miser, her troubled spirit haunted the moonlit banks of the Wansbeck on and near Meldon Bridge. One story identifies her as the daughter of a moneylender who, thanks to her great dowry, had married into the aristocracy. Her husband was Sir William Fenwick of Wallington and on his demise she took up residence at Hartington Hall. People said that she had dealings with the occult and had secreted away her vast treasure of gold and after her death wandered the earth in a variety of shapes checking her hidden hoards. She is also said to haunt a subterranean coach road.

A totally different tradition has it that Meg of Meldon was an old peasant woman who was smelly, evil-minded and a reputed witch. She lived beside a well in her village which was dry. People knew that she had once great wealth, but this she had hidden away. A poor cottager who lived nearby learned in a dream that Meg's well contained her great treasure and that …

> … it could be obtained at dead of night if one kept absolutely silent and accepted the help of a silent stranger who would help in the enterprise. He accordingly rose one night and by the light of the moon made his way to the well where indeed a stranger was waiting with long rope and grappling irons.

Together and silently, they threw the rope into the well. Together and silently they brought up a heavy bag from its bottom but as it neared the well edge the peasant could not restrain from shouting out delightedly, 'Now we have her!' The spell being broken, the stranger cackled with laughter and threw off her hood revealing herself as Meg, whereupon the bag with its gold treasure fell back into the well. The cottager ran off and never returned.

Crossroads, particularly lonely ones, were once used by communities as the burial places for 'the unholy' i.e. suicides, witches and hanged men and women. As can be imagined, stories of ghostly apparitions of the unquiet dead on or near crossroads were once plentiful. A very old belief was that the running of a stake through a dead body would prevent it 'walking' after death. How often this was done is not clear, but in 1823 the practice of resurrecting a body and driving a stake through it was forbidden by law. The *Denham Tracts* listing superstitions collected in the North East includes the following extract:

> A lady writes me: 'There is a ghost at Painters' gate, near Fowberry situated close to the cross roads between Wooler and Chatton, Fowberry and Lilburn. The ghost here is said to be a man on a dun-coloured horse.' Also at the cross roads at Lilburn, where a man riding with his head under his arm and a lady wringing her hands are said to be seen … a ghost used to frequent Weetwood Sandy Lane, and also Weetwood Bridge and the road approaching it from Wooler. If I remember right, some unhappy being … committed suicide, somewhere thereabouts.

Gallows and gibbets were once common sights in the North East; they were often set up at crossroads and shared some of the folklore attached to these unholy sites.

But Winter's Stob at Elsdon (*see* Gazetteer, chapter 13) and Andrew Mills' Stubb near Ferryhill were once both famous landmarks, not simply because they offered the vicarious thrill of seeing a dead man swinging either by the neck or in chains, but because it was superstitiously believed that wood taken from the stob was a cure-all for medical conditions, particularly toothache.

One and a half miles south-west of Aydon Castle, a medieval fortified manor house, is the ruins of an old castle now surrounded by a wood. The Revd O. Heslop, writing in the *Monthly Chronicle* (1888) informs us that a spectral army has been observed here several times by local people:

> The Hall is behind us, and its tragic story haunts the place. It is but a generation since the trampling of hoofs and the clatter of harness was heard on the brink of the step here, revealing to the trembling listeners that 'the Earl' yet galloped with spectral troops across the haugh. Undisturbed as the reverent hands of his people had laid him and his severed head, the earl himself had rested hardly in the little vault for a whole century; yet the troops have been seen by the country people over and over again as they swept and swerved through the dim mist of the hollow.

William Brockie records a story told to a Durham Sunday school teacher by one of the boys in the 1880s of another spectral army: 'I go there every evening to see the place; and if you walk nine times round the Cross, and then lay you head to the turf, you'll hear the noise of the battle and the clash of the armour'. The Battle of Neville's Cross was fought in October 1346.

Hare coursing was once very popular in the North East (it has been banned since 2002). In the past, hare coursing simply had two fast dogs pursuing the hare in the open countryside with the beaters following behind. The first dog to catch the hare was the winner: it was a test of speed and agility, with the dogs hunting by sight – and made even more exciting when the beaters turned it into a gambling event and placed bets on the dogs. The Revd Matthew Culley writing in the nineteenth century tells us:

> The village of Humbleton, not far from Wooler, where the famous battle was fought in 1403, is haunted by a ghost (of what sex I know not) in the form of a hare, which is hunted sometimes by the Wooler and Humbleton people – but is never killed.

Henderson recounts, 'Night after night … when it is sufficiently dark, the Headless Coach whirls along the rough approach to Langly Hall, near Durham, drawn by black and fiery steeds'.

FOUR

King Arthur & Other Heroes

Sewingshields Castle

The almost obliterated ruin of the medieval castle of Sewingshields (called 'the Castle of the Seven Shields' by Sir Walter Scott) is a couple of miles east of Housesteads and just to the north of Hadrian's Wall. Hodgson's *History of Northumberland* contains the following account:

Immemorial tradition has asserted that K A, his Q G, his court of lords and ladies, and his hounds were enchanted in some cave of the crags, or in hall below the castle of Sewingshields, and would continue entranced there till some one should first blow a bugle-horn that lay on a table near the entrance of the hall, and then with 'the sword of the stone' cut a garter also placed there beside it. But none had ever heard where the entrance to this enchanted hall was, till the farmer of Sewingshields, about fifty years since, was sitting knitting on the ruins of the castle, and his clew fell, and ran downwards through a rush of briars and nettles, as he supposed, into a deep subterranean passage. Full in the faith that the entrance to K A's hall was now discovered, he cleared the briary portal of its weeds and rubbish, and entering the vaulted passage, followed, in his darkling way, the thread of his clew. The floor was infested with toads and lizards; and the dark wings of bats disturbed by unhallowed intrusion flitted fearfully around him. At length his sinking courage was strengthened by a dim distant light, which, as he advanced, grew gradually brighter, till all at once, he entered a vast and vaulted hall, in the centre of which a fire without fuel, from a broad crevice in the floor, blazed with a high and lambent flame, that showed all the carved walls and fretted roof, and the monarch and his queen and court reposing around in a theatre of thrones and costly couches. On the floor beyond the fire, lay the faithful and deep toned pack of thirty couple of hounds; and on a table before it the spell-dissolving horn, sword and garter. The shepherd reverently but firmly grasped the sword, and as he drew it leisurely from its rusty scabbard the eyes of the monarch and his courtiers began to open, and they rose till they sat upright. He cut the garter; and as the sword was being slowly sheathed, the spell assumed its ancient power, and they all gradually sunk to rest; but not before the monarch had lifted up his eyes and hands and exclaimed:

O woe betide that evil day,
On which this witless wight was born,
Who drew the sword – the garter cut,
But never blew the bugle-horn

Terror brought on loss of memory, and the farmer was unable to give any correct account of his adventure or to find again the entrance to the enchanted hall.

Bruce's *Wallet-Book of the Roman Wall* mentions a further Sewingshields tradition:

To the north of Sewingshields, two strata of sandstone crop out … the highest points of each ledge are called the King and the Queen, from the following legend. King Arthur, seated on the furthest rock, was talking with his queen, who, meanwhile, was engaged in arranging her 'back hair'. Some expressions of the queen's having offended his majesty, he seized a rock which lay near him, and … threw it at her, a distance of about a quarter of a mile! The queen with great dexterity caught it upon her comb … the stone fell between them, where it lies to this very day, with the marks of the comb upon it, to attest the truth of the story. It probably weighs about twenty tons.

This legend follows several Welsh and Cornish traditions which depict Arthur, his queen and his followers as giants in the landscape and the common folklore motif of giants sitting on hilltops and throwing stones at each other.

Geoffrey Ashe mentions another strange Arthurian tradition from the 'neighbourhood' (exact source unspecified). This is of the visit of a northern chieftain to Arthur at Sewingshields who is given wealthy gifts. Arthur's sons, thinking the gifts too costly, waylay him and kill him at Cummings or Comyn's Cross, a standing stone two miles away on the edge of Haughton Common.

Bamburgh or Alnwick as Lancelot's Joyous Gard

Sir Thomas Malory, who probably fought in the Wars of the Roses in the Northumbria campaigns, reported that Lancelot's Joyous Gard was either Bamburgh or Alnwick. As the Celtic name for Bamburgh was 'Dinas Giuyardi', it is possible that a legendary connection was made with Lancelot in the medieval Romances when Lancelot was integrated as a Knight of the Round Table. According to Malory's composite fifteenth-century version, Lancelot frees prisoners from the Dolorous Gard, takes it over and re-names it the Joyous Gard, and lives with Guinevere there after abducting her. After becoming a monk hermit he is buried at Joyous Gard:

(Lancelot) prayed the bishop that his fellows might bear his body to Joyous Gard – some men say it was Alnwick, and some men say it was Bamburgh – 'howbeit,' said Sir Lancelot, 'me repenteth sore, but I made my vow some time, that in Joyous Gard I would be buried … And so within fifteen days, they came to Joyous Gard; and there they laid his corpse in

Bamburgh Castle; the site of Sir Lancelot's Joyous Gard. (Photo: Geoff Doel)

the body of the choir, and sang and read many psalters and prayers over him and about him … And right thus as they were at their service, there came Sir Ector de Maris that had seven years sought all England, Scotland and Wales, seeking his brother Sir Lancelot … Then went Sir Bors unto Sir Ector, and told him how there lay his brother Sir Lancelot, dead; and then Sir Ector threw his shield, sword and helm from him. And when he beheld Sir Lancelot's visage, he fell down in a swoon. And when he woke, it were hard any tongue to tell the doleful complaints that he made for his brother.

'Ah, Lancelot,' he said … 'thou were the courteoust knight that ever bore shield; and thou were the truest friend to thy lover that ever bestrode horse; and thou weret the truest lover of a sinful man that ever loved woman; and thou were the kindest man that ever struck with sword; and thou were the goodliest person that ever came among press of knights. And thou was the meekest man and the gentlest, that ever ate in hall among ladies, and thou were the sternest knight to thy mortal foe that ever put spear in the rest.

The year AD 547 is the legendary dating of the foundation of Ida's Anglian kingdom centred on Bamburgh. Its present name was given in the reign of Ida's grandson who named it for his wife Bebba. It was twice besieged by Penda the Mercian; on the first occasion he attempted to burn the fortress down at the base of the crag;,but the flames were driven back by the wind in answer to the prayers of St Aidan, who was then living as a hermit on Inner Farne.

Guy the Seeker

This legendary hero is in an enchanted sleep in a vault below Dunstanburgh Castle with his sword and horn; a similar tradition to King Arthur at Sewingshields. The traditional story is in the *Denham Tracts*, but was embroidered by the Gothic novelist M.G. Lewis in a poem called 'Guy the Seeker'.

The Earl of Derwentwater

There are many ghostly traditions about the Earl of Derwentwater who lived at Dilston Hall (now demolished) and was executed in 1716 because he joined the first Jacobite rebellion. There are traditions of omens of disaster, including very bright Northern Lights, which became known locally as 'Lord Derwentwater's Lights'. Formerly in the folklore of the area they had been called 'Merry Dancers' and 'Burning Spears'. Surtees in his *History of Durham* reports:

> The ignorant peasantry were not slow to receive the superstitious stories that were propagated on the occasion of the earl's death, and often has the rustic, beside the winter's

Dunstanburgh Castle. (From Sir Walter Scott's *Marmion*, 1855 edition)

The statue of Lord Collingwood, Rear Admiral at Trafalgar. (Photo: Geoff Doel)

hearth, listened to the fearful tale of how the spouts of Dilston Hall ran blood, and the very corn which was being ground came from the mill with a sanguine hue on the day the earl was beheaded.

Much memorabilia was preserved connected to him in the area. There are nineteenth-century traditions of a spectral Lord Derwentwater returning to Dilston leading a troop of ghostly soldiers and of his wife's ghost lamenting with a lamp at the top of the ruined castle tower.

Admiral Collingwood

Admiral Collingwood, whose statue surveys the entrance to the Tyne from Tynemouth, was Nelson's Rear Admiral at Trafalgar, who took command after Nelson's death. He features in a number of folksongs such as 'Drink Old England Dry' ('Twas Collingwood of high renown').

FIVE
SOME CANNY LASSES

According to R. Oliver Heslop, writing in 1889, the word 'canny' is 'sadly misunderstood by outsiders for many suppose it to have the same meaning as the better-known Scottish word which denotes cunning, craftiness or wariness. Heslop informs us that the Northumbrian 'canny' carries a totally different connotation for it is 'an embodiment of all that is kindly, good, and gentle'. Here then are some 'canny' lasses. The North abounds in legendary male figures but there are very few records of women's lives in the early historical accounts of Northumberland and Durham – with the notable exception of one or two royals who also happen to be saints.

The Venerable Bede familiarises us with a number of female saints' cults of the early period, but it is important to remember that as a monk and hagiographer, his concerns are with saintly behaviour and models and ideals of sanctity which are related to gender, and that in his writings he represents the Church which he has no wish to offend and the royal household which is supported by the Church.

Bede gave us the life of St Hild (614–680); she was of the Royal House of Edwin, and brought up in the Northumbrian court. These were the heady days of religious conversion when Paulinus sent from Kent brought Christianity (albeit briefly) to the North and conducted mass baptisms in the river beside the royal palace at Yeavering. These times of political stability were followed by years of warfare in the North and there is uncertainty about where Hild was sent for safety. Bede picks up her story when, on her return to Northumberland and influenced by the charismatic Irish ascetic Aidan, she takes the veil and becomes a nun. at Hartlepool

There are glimpses of a highly energetic and skilled administrator in Bede's description of her as abbess of the great double monastery at Whitby. Kings and princes sought her out, he informs us, attracted by her reputation for wisdom (more mundanely it could be argued that as her relatives they were simply paying her a visit). In legend she was said to have turned snakes into stone and is therefore frequently represented atop an ammonite. Yet another legend concerns the monastery at Harkness, which she founded in the last years of her life just fourteen miles from Whitby. On her death the bells of this institution rang out, tolled by angel hands.

Bede is careful not to offend the royal house of Northumbria when recounting the life of St Aebbe (615–683), venerated abbess and 'mother' of the double monastery

The Abbess Hild surrounded by her nuns.
(From Sir Walter Scott's *Marmion*, 1855
edition)

of Coldingham, and sister of the Northumbrian kings Oswald and Oswiu, for her
double monastery gained a reputation for moral laxity (though only after her death, it
must be said). Bede makes it clear that when it burned down it was regarded as divine
retribution.

Aebbe famously entertained St Cuthbert on her dramatic monastic site on the rocky
headland at *Urbs Coludi* from which he withdrew to immerse himself throughout the
night in the cold North Sea singing psalms. Local tradition asserts that as young woman
she had been shipwrecked on that beautiful stretch of the coast along with her retinue
of nuns after fleeing from a would-be suitor, Prince Aidan.

We have a third female royal saint's story related by Bede, that of the long-suffering
Queen Etheldreda (636–679), a would-be nun dedicated to chastity, who was shunted
into two marriages for dynastic reasons and ultimately fled to the Wash hotly pursued by
her second husband King Ecgfith of Northumbria who was desperate to consummate
the marriage. Bede does not give us the apocryphal stories that are told locally about
Etheldreda – that as she fled southwards and reached the headland Colbert's Head, her
husband and his soldiers closed in behind. To protect his virgin saint God caused the
North Sea to rise to an incredible height and flood the path to the headland. Ecgfrith
watched and waited for the ebb of the tide but when the water had not receded after
seven days he accepted that his wife was under supernatural protection and returned
home disconsolate. Etheldreda is often portrayed under a burgeoning tree or with a
flowering staff in her hand. This relates to the story of her relentless pursuit by Ecgfrith
when, overcome with weariness, Etheldreda pushed her staff into the ground and fell
into a deep sleep. When she awoke it was to discover that her staff had miraculously
rooted and produced branches and leaves. She left it there as a sign of God's providence
(uprooting it perhaps was problematic); it later grew into a great oak and was much
visited by pilgrims.

The site of St Aebbe's Monastery. (Photo: Geoff Doel)

As individuals and females these three women all gained a reputation for motherly love and concern for those in their charge and it is because of this that we call them 'canny'.

But their stories, factual and legendary, are only known because they were inadvertently involved in the male world of high politics and diplomacy. And their high rank along with their noteworthy piety as nuns and apparent brilliance in administration of their respective double monasteries deservedly make them figures of respect. If nothing else, they are fascinating embodiments of cultural modes of piety and moral excellence.

We now make an historic leap from the early days of Christianity to the North East at the time of the Jacobite Rising of 1715 and introduce a 'canny' lass of the Enlightened Age.

Dorothy Forster

A portrait of Dorothy Forster (1686–1767) hangs in Bamburgh Castle and shows us a very young, almost plain girl, her hair beautifully dressed, clad in silk and adorned with some very impressive jewellery. Perhaps it was painted too soon after her mother's premature death, when she and her brother Tom had been unofficially adopted by her aunt, Lady Crewe of Bamburgh Manor.

We know little about her childhood in Bamburgh Manor, but we do know a great deal about her family. Dorothy Forster came from a tough border-raiding family that originally owned lands and a pele tower in Adderstone near Norham. In the sixteenth century the family fortunes rocketed when John Forster was appointed Constable of Bamburgh Castle and granted a knighthood by Henry VIII. Sir John had at that point

Bamburgh Church – the last resting place of the Forsters. (Photo: Geoff Doel)

sufficient wealth from his own raiding exploits to buy from the king all the Augustinian lands in Bamburgh following the dissolution of the monasteries. Having thus acquired lands and title, Sir John's next step was to 'marry money', and he chose Jane Radclyffe, heiress to the Blanchland estate.

Sir John appears to have made a poor husband (he had numerous illegitimate offspring and was accounted a hard man), but he was a brilliant soldier and leader who consistently distinguished himself in numerous bloody border affrays and was rewarded with a string of titles, Warden of the Middle Marshes, Deputy Governor of Berwick and finally Deputy Warden of the East Marshes.

The fortunes of subsequent Adderstone-Forsters (as they had then become) peaked a second time during Elizabeth I's reign when Claudius Forster, grandson of Sir John, was appointed Constable of Bamburgh Castle and Sheriff of Northumberland. During the troubled times of the Civil War the family fortunes drastically declined, though the family continued to live in genteel elegance in Bamburgh linked by marriage ties to many of the great dynastic families in Northumberland, particularly the Radcliffes, whose head was the Earl of Derwentwater. In 1699, when the aunt of Dorothy Forster married Lord Crewe, the elderly Bishop of Durham, the family fortunes were ailing, but Lord Crewe was a wealthy man and obligingly bought the 'debt-ridden Bamburgh estates'. Five years later. Lady Crewe, beautiful, intelligent, happy in her marriage and without children of her own, took over her dead sister's children, Tom and Dorothy, and brought them to live with her in Bamburgh.

Brother Tom soon acquired all the hallmarks of an eighteenth-century country squire; he learned to hunt, shoot, fish and drink to excess; he also became MP for Northumberland. But many Northumbrian families were strong for the Stuart cause and when Queen Anne died in 1714 Tom, whose sympathies for The Stuart Heirs were

Denton Hall, the Northumbrian home of the Earl of Derwentwater. (From the *Monthly Chronicle* – 'North-Country Lore and Legends', 1887)

well known, was elected General of the Jacobite English army. The post was perhaps not well considered, for he was no soldier. After spending weeks recruiting across Northumberland with little success (Newcastle shut its gates on him), Tom's troops were joined by a Scottish force of Highlanders and moved south into England where they engaged with the English professional army at Preston. Though the Scots and Northumbrians fought bravely, Forster proved incompetent and made a number of bad decisions. The outcome was inevitable: 1,468 Jacobites were taken prisoner, 500 of them English. The Jacobite leaders, George Seton, 5th Earl of Winton, William Maxwell, 5th Earl of Nisdale, and James Radclyffe, 3rd Earl of Derwentwater and Tom Forster were taken to London. This is a contemporary description of how Tom along with rags and tatters of the Jacobite army were conducted through London:

> This week the prisoners were brought to town from Preston: they came in with their arms tied and their horses (whose bridles were taken off) each led by a soldier. The mob insulted them terribly, carrying a warming-pan in front of them and saying a thousand barbarous things, which some of the prisoners returned with spirit.

As a result of this battle many clansmen were transported to America, while Seton, Maxwell and Derwentwater were imprisoned in the Tower and sentence to be executed for treason. Tom was imprisoned in Newgate Goal in London, also under sentence of death.

It is at this point that Dorothy Foster comes into the story and where she transmutes into the 'canny lass' of such renown and a figure of folklore with a cluster of legends attached to her name. Dorothy had the spirit of her border forefathers. She was determined not to abandon her brother. She appealed to every male Northumbrian relative in turn and appeared astonished that no one was prepared to get involved in such a potentially volatile situation. Everything seemed stacked against her: her sympathetic aunt had died; her uncle Lord Crewe, now well into his eighties, had retired to his estate in Northamptonshire; she herself had little personal fortune; no carriage was at her disposal to get her to the capital. There was also the fact that winter had set in and deep snows were blocking the roads. What did she do?

No one really knows. If one accepts the legend (and there are several variants) she set off from Bamburgh on horseback in a snowstorm riding pillion behind the local blacksmith. Some nineteenth-century accounts, fearing some impropriety in the relationship, call him a cousin. The pair made firstly for Northamptonshire and Lord Crewe – and it is thought they were well received. After that they pressed on to London where, by a ruse or by bribery or both, she helped her brother escape from Newgate. Perhaps she found that he was already being helped, for the Jacobites had friends in high places in the city; both Seton and Maxwell escaped from the Tower while Tom was got out of Newgate. Derwentwater was not so lucky and was later beheaded on Tower Hill.

Tom fled to France and died there in 1738 when his body was shipped back to Bamburgh; his body lies in the family crypt of St Aidan's Church.

Dorothy's body lies alongside that of her brother's. She died in 1767 having married a local man, John Armstrong – the romantically inclined assert he was the blacksmith who conducted the canny lass of Bamburgh to London.

Miss Bell

In the early nineteenth century many qualified seamen aged between eighteen and forty-five were press-ganged by the Royal Navy during the period of the Napoleonic wars as a means of crewing warships. By law, the length of service of a pressed man could extend up to five years, but there was the proviso that a man couldn't be pressed twice. The following account comes from the *Monthly Chronicle* for 1891, but it is referring to an earlier period. All we know about the nameless young woman is that she was presumably called Miss Bell and was a quirky, audacious girl who despite all the odds and because of her love and loyalty for her brother, dared to challenge the system – and cheekily succeeded:

> In 1813 (February 10) a sailor named Bell belonging to the Close, Newcastle, was impressed, and safely lodged in the house of rendezvous. In the evening his sister, a young woman under twenty, formed the resolution of attempting his rescue, and for that purpose, went to tale 'a long farewell' of her brother, who was to be sent to his tender in the morning. She was readily admitted to an interview, but, in order to prevent the impossibility of escape, brother and sister were bolted and barred for a few minutes, in a room by themselves. During this short space, they managed to exchange clothes, and on the door being opened, the young man 'snivelling and piping his eye,' walked off unmolested in female attire, while his sister remained to fill the situation of a British tar. 'It would be difficult,' says a writer in the *European Magazine* (who tells the story), 'to describe the rage and disappointment of the gang on discovering how they had been duped; and crowds of persons went to see the

heroine, who received several pounds from the spectators as a reward for her intrepidity and affection. She was soon restored to her liberty by order of the magistrates.

Peggy Brown from Cresswell

In 1851, the Duke of Northumberland offered a prize of one hundred guineas for the best design of a purpose-built coble that could be used as a lifeboat, and promised to equip the Northumbrian coast with lifeboats and rockets at his own expense. Ironically that very same year saw a great storm in which ten fishermen from Newbiggin were lost. As a direct result of the competition (and the storm) the duke provided Newbiggin, Cullercoats and Warkworth with lifeboats and lifeboat stations. Newbiggin, which is mentioned in the following extract, is the oldest operational boathouse in Britain and was fully functional by 1854. Peggy Brown is a delightful heroine and really canny lass. The middle-class Victorian readers of the *Folklore Journal* in which the extract appears probably saw her as a poorly educated fisher girl, but she is resourceful, courageous, self -sacrificing and good. This account is from the late nineteenth century:

> Our coast is often a scene of shipwreck. One bitter night in January in the 1870s a schooner crashed on the reef at Snab Point There was no lifeboat then and the Cresswell fishermen had been unable to make their return. The women and girls of the village were out on the beach and could hear the cries of the crew. One gallant-hearted girl named Peggy Brown cried out, 'If I thowt she could hing on a bit, I wad be away for the lifeboat.' Between Cresswell and Newbiggin, the nearest lifeboat station, the Lyne Burn runs into the sea and spreads widely out over the sands; and the older people told Peggy she could never cross the burn in the dark. She set off, however, the thought of the drowning men hastening her on. For four miles she made her way in the storm and the darkness, partly along the shore, scrambling over rocks and wading waist-deep through the Lyne Burn and one or two places where the waves had driven up far up the sands, and partly across Newbiggin Moor, where the icy wind tore at her in her drenched clothing. She pressed on, however, and managed to reach the coxswain's house and give her message. The lifeboat was immediately run out, and the men reached the wreck in time to save all the crew except one, who had been washed overboard.

Grace Darling

Grace Horsley Darling (1815–1842) is the archetypical canny lass and a much-admired heroine whose reputation and legend were substantially established by the newly bourgeoning newspaper industry in the early nineteenth century. In addition to extensive contemporary media coverage she was lauded by two of the greatest Victorian poets of the day, Algernon Swinburne (1837–1909) and William Wordsworth (1770–1850) who wrote verses in her honour. Both these great men had links with the North; Swinburne's grandfather was Sir John Swinburne of Capheaton Hall in Northumberland, and William Wordsworth received an honorary doctorate from Durham University in 1838 just four years before Grace's death.

The Longstone Light, home of Grace Darling. (Photo: Geoff Doel)

Grace embodies everything that makes a romantic heroine. First of all her name was charming and suggestive of virtue and loving humanity. Secondly she was touchingly young when she was called to undertake a courageous and daring action. Thirdly she lived in an extraordinarily beautiful and romantic remote location – the Farne Islands where her father was keeper of the Longstone Light. The paparazzi would later seize on these romantic ideals as newsworthy, but the reality is that she was a very 'ordinary' person who found herself in extraordinary and dangerous circumstances and rose magnificently to the occasion. An ability to face danger with a sense of confidence and fearlessness was not expected from a woman at this period. And her great deed has granted her immortality of a sort – there is an excellent and modern museum celebrating her life and her heroic deed in the village of Bamburgh.

Grace's early life was spent on two very small rocky islands – first Brownsman then Longstone – off the coast of Northumberland where her father William was keeper of the light. There were nine children in all and Grace was educated at home and helped her father with his duties. This is an area that has always been dangerous for shipping due to sunken rocks and dangerous currents but the family regularly commuted between the islands and the coast by coble (a clinker-built open fishing boat that usually takes three men to man) and Grace had the very best teachers concerning practical knowledge of seamanship.

In the early hours of 7 September 1838, Grace was on watch. Visibility was almost nil and the Farnes had been lashed all night by a hurricane. During the night a steamer called the *Forfarshire* with a cargo of machinery and sixty passengers and crew on board had passed the Farnes and came abreast of Berwick. The Captain was a Tyneside man, Captain Humble. Unable to enter the harbour because the sea had become furious and the engines ceased to work, they were compelled to pull back southwards. Early in the morning they foundered on one of the Farne's rocky outcrops known as the Harkers. In a force gale the steamer broke in half and half sunk with massive loss of life.

An engraving of Grace Darling, 1852.

The Rescue. (From Eva Hope's *Grace Darling*)

William Darling. (From Eva Hope's *Grace Darling*)

Above: Grace Darling's Tomb. (From Eva Hope's *Grace Darling*)

Left: The Survivors of the wreck of the Forfarshire. (From Eva Hope's *Grace Darling*)

As soon as Grace was able to discern the wreck of the *Forfarshire* on Big Harker and saw that there were survivors, she and her father pushed out to sea in their coble. The wind and waves were so high that Grace's mother's help was needed to even launch the boat into the sea. Father and daughter rowed for a mile, keeping to the lee side of the islands for shelter until parallel with Big Harker. Grace then held the coble steady as best she could while William leaped onto the rock. Eight men (including some crew members) and one woman with dead children in her arms were clinging to the rock. All were brought back safely to the lighthouse in two stages by William and two of the shipwrecked seamen while Grace and her mother saw to the welfare of those who had survived.

Grace and her father were not the only heroes of the day. Brother William Coxon of the North Sunderland lifeboat succeeded in reaching Longstone with his crew. It was a magnificent effort and feat of seamanship, but because the lighthouse was crowded with survivors, the entire lifeboat crew were forced to shelter in the cold washhouse for two days until the storm abated.

The first account of the dramatic rescue appeared in the *Newcastle Chronicle*. The story was then copied in all the newspapers (often with accompanying drawings of Grace or the Farne Islands, for the camera had not yet been invented) and Grace became the darling of the nation. Sadly, Grace only survived four more years, for she died of tuberculosis in 1842.

Bessie Surtees

The elopement of pretty Bessie Surtees the young Newcastle heiress and John Scott a penniless student is an eighteenth-century story of forbidden love, all the better for having a happy ending.

The elopement of John Scott and Bessie Surtees, 1772. (From the *Monthly Chronicle* – 'North-Country Lore and Legend', 1890)

Today, choosing a marriage partner is considered a private expression of love between a couple, but in the eighteenth century marriages were often contracted, particularly in aristocratic circles and there was no period of courtship. Young men and women were often introduced to each other with the cultural assumption that their marriage was to be arranged by their respective parents for the mutual benefit of both families. In a rich banking family such as the Surtees where great wealth had been amassed there was always an obligation to marry well and certainly into another wealthy family, if not the aristocracy. Bessie Surtees was by all accounts a personable and extremely pretty young woman and she had the misfortune to fall in love with a young man whom her father heartily disliked. Bessie was well aware that society considered it her duty to obey her father in all things and that he had a perfect right to veto the match and withhold her dowry but she was in love …

Aubone Surtees and his family lived in a great timbered house in Sandhill, Newcastle-upon-Tyne. This and the adjacent beautiful Jacobean building are still standing on the Newcastle-upon-Tyne quayside. Bessie and Jack Scot a bright but penniless student fell desperately in love. When Bessie was sent to stay with her aunt in Sedgefield, Durham, Jack tracked her down and relentlessly pursued and courted her. But Aubone Surtees had a grudge against Jack's father, a Newcastle keel owner and coal dealer and was adamant that the match would never take place. He kept them apart until 1772 when, at the dead of night, a young gentleman called Wilkinson (Jack's best friend and confidant) tiptoed up to the Surtees house carrying a long ladder and set it under Bessie's bedroom window. While Bessie was shakily climbing down from her first-floor bedroom window Jack was awaiting her impatiently with a post-chaise. The couple fled to Scotland where they were married the following morning at Black Shields and by every account 'lived very happily ever after'.

William Scott was generous to his son and presented him with £2,000 on his marriage and £1,000 some four years later. After a wait of two and a half years, old Aubone decided to 'extend to his delinquents an ostensible forgiveness'.

Jack not only successfully completed his studies at Oxford, but ultimately went into the law where he carved a brilliant career for himself, becoming (twice) Lord High Chancellor of England. In 1821 he was further rewarded by being created an earl. His love for Bessie is said never to have diminished and today there is a blue glass which marks Bessie's bedroom and a commemorative brass tablet recording her story in the Sandhill house.

Dolly Peel

In 1989, a statue was erected to Dolly (Dorothy) Peel (1783–1857), a locally famous South Shields fishwife. It commands a magnificent view over the south Tyne. Dolly wears a distinctive 'fisher-girl' costume – similar to that adopted by forces of itinerant fisher-girls up and down the east coast everywhere until the late Victorian period. It consisted of a long very full skirt worn over one or two petticoats, a bodice, an apron and a shawl. Some communities such as the Cullercoats fishwives individualised their costume and wore a distinctive blue serge jacket and a black straw bonnet. If they did not work with the 'gangs' on the quayside fisher wives such as Dolly worked for their husbands, prepared their man's bait, carried his gear to the boats, and when the boats came in took laden creels on their backs, and hawked the catch throughout Tyneside.

Dolly was well known in her community and highly thought of. In later life she ran a pub on the shoreline and was not averse to illicit trading. She had other unexpected abilities; she was by all accounts a brilliant story teller and a singer song writer. Perhaps nowadays she would have run a folk club.

But even more extraordinary than all of this, Dolly was one of those rare females who had served as a 'Female Tar' on board a man-of-war during the Napoleonic Wars. She had on a number of occasions been obliged to hide her husband from the Press Gang but when both her husband and son were impressed by the Royal Navy during the Napoleonic Wars she took it on herself to put on man's attire and secrete herself on board their ship. She was discovered by the captain who could have put her ashore but who instead decided to used her services as a nurse in the infirmary and in attendance to the ship's doctor. By all accounts she did a very good job and served for the duration of the war.

A statue of Dolly Peel, South Shields, June 2008. (Photo: Geoff Doel)

Cuddy's Folk
& Legends of
St Cuthbert

Affectionately known as 'Cuddy', no northern saint has been more praised or written about than St Cuthbert, who is regarded as the benefactor and protector of his people – hence, 'Cuddy's Folk'. It is also possible that no English saint has created more folklore. The massive romanesque cathedral of Durham was erected in the post-conquest period to house a monastic community created in the saint's honour, and also as an immense reliquary to house the miracle-working bones of the saint. The age in which the saint lived, the seventh century, was a time of turmoil and radical change in the North; the Irish Church, with the agreement of the Northumbrian king, and staffed and directed from Iona, was establishing its own unique form of Christianity and religious practices in the northern territories.

The great St Aidan, having created a monastic missionary centre on the causeway island of Lindisfarne – later known as Holy Island – set up the network of satellite monasteries staffed by monks needed to convert the vast and still pagan North. Cuthbert was born in Northumbria (but in what is now known as lowland Scotland) and was of 'early English' (Germanic) parentage. As a young shepherd, inspired by tales from his Celtic Christian foster-mother, he began to engage in prayer with the 'new' God. Soon he was experiencing visions – the first was of Aidan's soul ascending into the heavens attended by angels. Obliged to do military service in his lord's wars, he returned battle weary, and, aged just seventeen, went to the monastery at Melrose, one of the mission stations created by Aidan, and was received into the brotherhood. So began Cuthbert's life as a monk.

Soon he was actively engaged in the penitential austerity encouraged by the Irish Church that saw self-sacrifice and death as the way to God. Even after the Synod of Whitby, which introduced Roman Church Rule into Britain, and which had him created prior of the Lindisfarne community, he continually withdrew from the brethren to the tiny island of Hob Thrush to isolate himself for God. Then followed eleven long

Lindisfarne Priory and Church. (Photo: Geoff Doel)

years as a hermit on Inner Farne where, on a massive piece of basalt rock, he constructed a hermitage and withdrew from the world.

The first (anonymous) biography of Cuthbert was written in Lindisfarne and wrongly described Cuthbert as an Irish nobleman. The second and third, written by the eminent scholar Bede, himself an English monk in the Anglo-Saxon religious communities of Monkwearmouth and Jarrow, were carefully researched and lay emphasis on what distinguishes Cuthbert (apart from his undoubted piety) – his racial stock; he is the first great English saint of the North.

Cuthbert & the Pictish Princess

This apocryphal but oft-told story of Cuthbert and the princess is impossible to date, although the twelfth century might be a good guess as one of its motifs, the earth vacuuming a malefactor into hell, was regularly used in saints' tales at this period. It may have served as an *exemplum* of why Cuthbert prohibited women entering his shrine.

As Bede tells us, Cuthbert as a young man had functioned as a hermit missionary in the North and worked amongst the Pictish tribes. Bede, however, does not relate the legendary story that follows. It appears that a Pictish king had been informed of his unmarried daughter's pregnancy and in a great rage had the girl dragged before him and bade her confess who the father was. Unwilling to reveal that it was an unsuitable young man the girl outrageously claimed that she had been seduced by the physical beauty and seductive words of Cuthbert. The saint was devastated by the accusation. Dissolving into tears and lamentations, he called upon God to prove his innocence and before the assembled tribe the truth was soon made known for with a great noise the earth began to split asunder and a great crack appeared before the princess's feet. Great hissings were heard and sulphur clouds issued from the fissure; then the lying girl with piteous shrieks and horrid moans was sucked into hell. The father not unnaturally was appalled. He begged Cuthbert to save his child. Cuthbert graciously assented to do this, but 'on condition that from thence, no woman should come near him. And so it came to pass that the king did not suffer any woman to enter into any church dedicated to that saint, which to this day is duly observed'.

St Peter's Church, Monkwearmouth,
where Bede was brought as a boy.
(From the *Monthly Chronicle* – 'North
Country Lore and Legends', 1891)

Cuddy's Beads

These are fossils, circular crinoid columnals, hollow inside, segments of the 'stems' of carboniferous crinoids. They are often washed out of the rock and onto beaches. Locally they are known as St Cuthbert's Beads, or Cuddy's Beads, and in the medieval period they were collected and threaded as rosary beads. An old legend says that the saint laboriously forged the fossils on his anvil on Hob Thrush, a little rock off Holy Island on the Northumbrian coast, where he had an early hermitage:

> *On a rock, by Lindisfarne,*
> *St Cuthbert sits and toils to frame*
> *The sea-born beads that bear his name*

The Cuddy Ducks

Inner Farne is the breeding grounds for eider ducks. These were the saint's 'special' birds; they kept him company when he toiled in his little fields as a hermit, and lay quietly near his feet when he prayed.

Legends of the Travelling Coffin

Sir Walter Scott gives a résumé of the lively posthumous journeys of the saint's miracle-working bones and relics, including his stone boat, once they were uprooted from

Lindisafrne in his notes to 'Marmion', which are quoted below. It is to be noted that even when he was dead Cuthbert continued to keep in dynamic contact through dreams and visions with those who were toting his remains all round Northumbria in a wooden coffin. If they were in any doubt of his wishes he simply rooted his coffin to the ground and the monks could not budge it:

His body was initially brought to Lindisfarne, where it remained until a descent of the Danes, about 793, when the monastery was nearly destroyed. The monks fled to Scotland, with what thy deemed their chief treasure: the relics of St Cuthbert. The saint was, however, a most capricious fellow traveller, like Sinbad's Old Man of the Sea he journeyed upon the shoulders of his companions. They paraded him through Scotland for several years, and came as far west as Whit Horn, in Galloway, whence they attempted to sail for Ireland, but boats were driven back by tempests. Cuthbert at length made a halt at Norham; from thence he went to Melrose where he remained stationary for a short time, and then caused himself to be launched upon the Tweed in a stone coffin, which landed him at Tilmouth in Northumberland. Cuthbert wandered into Yorkshire and at last made a long stay at Chester-le-Street, to which the bishop's See was transferred. When the Danish threat increased, the monks removed Cuthbert to Ripon for a season; and it was on their return from thence to Chester-le-Street, that, when they reached a hill called Wrdelaw (thought to be Warden Law, near Houghton-le-Spring), the shrine came to a miraculous halt. During the three days fast and vigil which the monks endured to find why their saint had rooted himself to the spot, one of their number experienced a vision in which he heard a voice ordering him to 'take the body to Dunholme'.

A book entitled the *Ancient Rites of Durham* explains that the guardians were distraught because they had no idea where Dunholme was. 'See their goode fortune!' says the book, for 'as they were goinge, a woman that lacked her cowe, did call aloude

The Guardians of St Cuthbert carrying the saint's coffin with its sacred inclusions throughout the land, seeking a permanent home. (From Sir Walter Scott's *Marmion*, 1855 edition)

St Cuthbert's Cross and the Dun Cow, Durham Cathedral. (From the *Monthly Chronicle* = 'North-Country Lore and Legend', 1890)

to hir companion to know if shee did not see hir, who answered with a loud voice that hir cowe was in Dunholm.' This was the end of the journey for the monks for they had found a resting place for their precious load, and it was here that Durham Cathedral was subsequently built.

In a surprising turn of events, the Hereditary Guardians of St Cuthbert were declared unworthy of their sacred position and their precious load was taken from them soon after the Conquest. The *Monthly Chronicle* for the year 1889 gives an account of the political take-over:

> Soon after the Conquest in 1081, William de Carileph, Bishop of Durham, found the Church of St Cuthbert (established by his predecessor, Aldhune, in 998) occupied by secular clergy, who had wives and families, and whose lives as one chronicler suggests, were far from exemplary. The bishop, therefore, removed them from the cathedral, giving them prebendaries in the churches of Auckland, Darlington, Norton and Heighington and filling their places at Durham, by removing thither the monks of Jarrow and Monkwearmouth. This was the year 1083. Norton them became a collegiate church.

Two milkmaids and a cow are sculpted on the outside of the turret at the north end of the Chapel of the Nine Altars at Durham Cathedral to illustrate the legend of the body of the saintly Cuthbert finding a permanent home in Durham.

Cuthbert's Stone Boat

According to a nineteenth century account, 'the coffin is finely shaped, 10ft long, 3½ft and in diameter, and only four inches thick; so that with very little assistance, it might certainly have floated. It still lies, or at least did so a few years ago, in two pieces, beside the ruined Chapel of Tilmouth'.

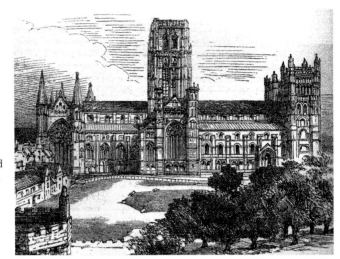

Durham Cathedral, where the body of Cuthbert was enshrined and visited by countless pilgrims in the Middle Ages. (From the *Monthly Chronicle –* 'North-Country Lore and Legend', 1890)

Cuthbert & William the Conqueror

Simeon of Durham tells us that William I sent precious jewels to the new cathedral for the ' adornment of Cuthbert's image' and then came to Durham in person to pay homage to the saint. Here fact and fiction part company. Some stories say that the saint was so incensed by the visit that he inflicted an unaccountable and unbearable heat on the Conqueror so that he fled and could find no relief until he reached the south.

Cuthbert the Misogynist

In the twelfth century Cuthbert's shrine was a magnet for male pilgrims because it was attested that Cuthbert was a feared misogynist who had made it very clear that female pilgrims should be denied access to his shrine. Whether this so-called aversion to womankind had its roots in Bede or was a myth propagated by the Durham monks for pragmatic reasons – Durham was after all a male-only monastic foundation and Cuthbert's shrine lay adjacent to the choir where the monks were required to spend a large part of their day in the *opus dei* – it became the rule that women should be kept away from the monastic part of the church and their movement within the cathedral severely restricted in order not to compromise the monks' enclosure.

It was accepted however that female pilgrims would naturally wish to visit so sacred a spot and should have some reward for undertaking long and difficult pilgrimages; there was too an obligation for the bishop to provide a chapel where female pilgrims could pray and hear mass 'for their comfort and consolation'. Fiscal consideration may also have played a part, for denying women access to the shrine incurred a loss of revenue in pilgrims' offerings. Hugh de Pudsey accordingly ordered a Lady Chapel to be built at the east angle of the cathedral. After a false start, the builders declared the site unsuitable and a new site was elected – the west end of the church now known as the Galilee Chapel, built in 1154. From here women pilgrims could progress into the great nave of the cathedral church, but only for a few feet, for they were soon halted at a demarcation line of frosterley marble. Sumption tells us that 'muscular stewards' were employed by Durham Cathedral to keep disorderly pilgrims in order.

Cuthbert's legendary aversion to women was propagated in a number of once well-known medieval stories. Two of these relate to the cathedral cemetery which was at one point being used by local women out on their housewifely errands as a shortcut to the town or market, something that seemed to offend Cuthbert.

Sungeona, wife of Gamelus, trying to avoid puddles in the street on a rainy Durham day, picked her way though the cathedral cemetery. Sadly, this so enraged the saint that she died that night.

Another Durham woman, whose name was not given, was unwise enough to use the cemetery as a shortcut to the market place. Some time later unknown forces 'so affected' her that she was driven to commit suicide.

Another legend claimed that the ghost of an indignant Cuthbert had bodily risen from his shrine when, in 1333, Queen Philippa joined her husband Edward III in the prior's apartments within the monastery. The queen, exhausted after a long journey, was already undressed and in bed when one of the senior monks, indignant that any female should spend even one night in the cloistral quarters when it was expressly forbidden by Cuthbert, demanded that the queen be ejected. Philippa still in her night attire was therefore rushed across to the castle where a bed was quickly prepared for her. Only then did Cuthbert deign to return to his shrine.

Simeon of Durham (writing c. 1100) has two stories of how St Cuthbert severely punished two audacious women who had attempted to gain admittance to his precious sanctuary. One was Judith, wife of Earl Tostig, who, when she tried to cross over the threshold of the shrine chapel, had been paralysed at the door by the offended saint. Cuthbert had similarly zapped another girl, a chambermaid in the retinue of King David of Scotland, who had hoped to slip in unnoticed with the King's male party.

A few impudent but courageous young women dressed up as men in an attempt to penetrate this hallowed male sanctum. In 1417, two young serving women from Newcastle-upon-Tyne disguised themselves as men and tried to 'blend in' with an all-male pilgrim band that were being conducted round the church and shrine. Sadly they were soon detected and ignominiously dragged before the bishop. Their punishment was an exercise in public humiliation. They were ordered to dress up in their male attire and process round the parish after which they had to stand before the congregation during the service in their parish church St Nicholas and All Saints, Newcastle-upon-Tyne. Hundreds turned out to watch and jeer – or was it cheer?

Cuthbert & the Standard

The Middle Ages were uneasy times and the great lords of the North and their standing armies were frequently engaged in bloody warfare. Even though dead and enshrined in his great cathedral, Cuthbert, in order to protect his city and his special 'folk', would communicate with his monks through dreams. In 1346 when King David of Scotland had burnt Lanercost Priory, sacked Hexham Priory and moved within a mile or two of Durham, battle seemed inevitable. To protect his people the saint invaded the dreams of his monks and ordered them to extemporise a standard by fastening the 'corporal' (a cloth which he had personally used to cover the chalice of the Eucharist, and which was imbued with holy virtue) to the shaft of a spear. Thus fashioned, 'Cuthbert's Standard' was duly carried into battle at the Battle of Neville's Cross and ensured victory. To acknowledge their gratitude to Cuthbert, 'the victors repaired to the Cathedral for the succour of the mighty saint beneath whose holy banner they had fought'. They had lost comparatively few of their rank.

Cuthbert & the Sanctuary Knocker

In the Middle Ages all churches possessed the privilege of sanctuary though some churches to a much greater degree than others. The cathedral of Durham was one of these more favoured churches because it contained the shrine of St Cuthbert. Criminals 'that fled thither besought the immunity of the said church and the liberty of St Cuthbert,' and the saint graciously extended his protection to the miscreants.

When a claimant reached the cathedral (guided by series of wooden crosses that flanked the main roads that led to the church) he proceeded to the north door and knocked for admission. Day and night there were monks according to the Ancient Rites of Durham 'that did lie always in two chambers over the said north door' and 'straightway they were letten in, at any hour of the night'.

Once the claimant was in, a monk would run to the Galilee Chapel and toll its bell to indicate that someone had taken sanctuary. The prior was at the same time informed of the culprit's entrance and warned him that he should keep within the limits of sanctuary, which in the monastery extended to the limits of the churchyard. He was also required in the presence of witnesses to make a full and explicit statement of the crime he had committed giving names, dates, place and in the case of murder naming the murder implement. He was then dressed in a black gown, on the left shoulder of which was a yellow cross called St Cuthbert's cross. Sanctuary was afforded for a period of thirty-seven days during which he was furnished with meat, drink and bedding at the expense

The Sanctuary Knocker on the north door of Durham Cathedral. (Photo: Archie Turnbull)

Seeking sanctuary at Durham Cathedral. (From the *Monthly Chronicle* – 'North-Country Lore and Legend', 1890)

of the convent. His sleeping place was a little room within the church adjoining the Galilee door on the south side.

During the time of sanctuary the refugee was encouraged to settle with his adversaries. If he failed to do this he was required to appear, clothed in sackcloth, before the coroner, confess his crime and agree to quit the realm. The usual form of abjuration was as follows:

> Because I have done such evils in his land, I do abjure the land of our lord the king, and I shall haste me towards he port of [xxxx] and that I shall not go out of the highway; [but will] diligently seek for passage and that I will tarry there but one flood, and ebb if I can have passage: and unless I can have it in such place, I will go very day into the seas up to my knees, assaying to pass over: and unless I can do this within forty days, I will put myself again into the church … so God help me and his holy judgement

As he travelled on his way to the port appointed for his departure (carrying a white wooden cross), the culprit was conducted from place to place by the constables of the different parishes though which he passed.

A sanctuary book records that 331 criminals sought refuge in Cuthbert's greatest church between 1464 and 1524, most of them murderers and all of them male. Other criminals seeking sanctuary included numerous cattle and horse thieves; debtors, prison breakers and house burglars.

A number of kings visited Cuthbert's shrine in Durham. Cnut shaved his head, trimmed his beard and removed his shoes in order to undertake a five-mile penitential walk to the shrine in its pre-Norman church. Henry VIII visited the shrine in September 1448 then had acts passed severely abridging the right of sanctuary. These were further curtailed in 1603 and then totally abolished in 1624.

Norham Church possessed the privilege of thirty-seven days' sanctuary.

An engraving of Durham Cathedral on its high site overlooking the River Wear. (From Sir Walter Scott's *Marmion*, 1855)

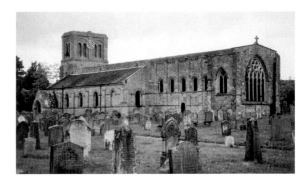

Norham Church, one of the northern sanctuary churches in the past. (Photo: Geoff Doel)

Cuthbert's Healing Shrine

For several hundreds of years this brought thousands of pilgrims to Durham. Through the sanctity of numerous other relics, and the *virtus* exuded by the holy bones of Cuthbert, Oswald and Bede, thousands of miraculous cures were claimed to have been effected, all of which were carefully recorded by such monks as Reginald of Durham. The shrine itself was described by a contemporary as:

> … exalted with most curious workmanship of fine and costly green marble, all limed and gilt with gold, having four seats or places convenient under the shrine for the pilgrims or lame men sitting on their knees to lean and rest on, at the time of their devout offerings and fervent prayers to God and holy St Cuthbert for his miraculous relief and succour; which being never wanting, made the shrine to be so richly invested that it was estimated to be one of the most sumptuous monuments in England, so great were the offering and jewels bestowed upon it, and no less the miracles that were done by it.

The shrine had a rich gilt cover surmounted by protective dragons; it was raised by means of a pulley and rope, and 'its lifting rang six silver bells'. It was lifted twice a day, during Matins and at evensong. Precious offerings in the way of jewels were actually hung on the shrine, lesser offerings enclosed within a nearby feretory:

> And when they had maid there praiers & dyed ofer any thing to it, if yt weare eithr gould sylver or Jewels streighte way it was hounge on y shrine. And yf yt wye any other thing, as unicorne horne, Eliphant tooth or such like thynge then yt was howng within the fereture at y end of ye shrine, and when they had maid there praiers, the Clarke di let down ye cover therof & did lock yt at very corner.

For reasons of security a twenty-four-hour watch was kept on the shrine by a recluse whose anchorhold was built high up between two pillars on the north side of the choir and which overlooked the shrine.

Cuthbert's shrine was dismantled at the Dissolution and legend has it that the hiding place of Cuthbert's body (said to be under the floor of the actual shrine), was entrusted only to three monks of the original order; 'whenever one died, so they entrusted the secret of the burial place to one other'.

SEVEN

HERMITS

Northumbria has numerous fascinating eremitical sites principally because of their associations with early Irish missionary activities in the North. The hermits of the early Church were considered holy elite; they were the 'athletes of Christ' and a great deal of folklore has grown up round them. It is impossible to know why so many men chose to adopt this harsh penitential life-style but it is suggested that some isolated themselves through 'weariness of the world, and a longing desire to merit transference to a better, through a persistent course of austerity and sacrifice'. Their hermitages were usually isolated spots, rocks out at sea, causeway islands or sea caves; their solitary abode was often referred to as a 'wilderness' or 'desert place', a reference to the cells of the Desert Fathers whose life-style they were emulating. It is important to know that the early Church made provision for their inclusion and direction. The great Cuthbert, for example, was attended by monks from Lindisfarne who helped him construct his cell and oratory and regularly rowed out to his desert hermitage on Inner Farne. Godric of Finchale was often visited by his bishop.

In the late medieval period many men and also women in the North became anchorites. This is a term which is often used as a synonym for hermit, but there is a difference. Anchorites and anchoresses lived in an 'anchorhold' or 'anchorage', usually a purpose-built two-roomed apartment constructed against a church. One room was for living in, while the other was for private devotions. After a special ceremony and blessing by the bishop the anchorite was 'walled' into this dwelling and never again left it. After death, they were buried under the floor of the oratory. In their living room was a small window (hagioscope) which permitted the anchorite to see one of the altars in the church. A second small curtained window gave access to the outside world. A servant was usually appointed to pass food through the window, bring water, take away slops etc. Passers-by could converse with the anchorite through this window though 'gossip' was discouraged.

The Reformation brought an end to this reclusive religious lifestyle.

Coquet Island where Henry the Dane (d. 1127) lived as a hermit and was visited by those who believed he was prophetic and 'could read the secrets of hearts'. The island had a community of monks in the age of Bede and was where St Cuthbert met Elfleda, Abbess of Whitby. (Photo: Geoff Doel)

Tynemouth Priory ruins. (From Sir Walter Scott's *Marmion*, 1855 edition)

An interior view of Tynemouth Priory ruins. Henry the Dane's body was brought from Coquet and was buried in the priory sanctuary alongside that of the priory's patron, St Oswin. (From the *Monthly Chronicle* – 'North-Country Lore and Legends', 1887)

The Chester-le-Street Anchorites

Chester-le-Street boasts one of the finest extant anchorite cells that can be visited anywhere in Britain. Here the incumbent at his own behest was walled into a two-roomed cell attached to the side of the church and which he never left. Here he led a life of prayer and contemplation, his only access to the outside world being a small squint window which offered him a view of an altar within the church, and a tiny window near to the west door where local people could approach him for spiritual advice. A servant brought him food and drink and took away all waste.

The Hermit of Coquet Island

This was the site of a small Benedictine monastery as early as 684 and the scene of an important interview between Elfleda, the abbess of Whitby, and St Cuthbert. One of the monks from Tynemouth Priory, Henry the Dane, retired here as hermit. His body was taken back to his community in Tynemouth Priory for burial and he was accounted a saint.

Godric of Finchale

Today there are the remains of medieval buildings standing on an isolated spot on the banks of River Wear on the site where Godric constructed his hermitage in the early twelfth century.

At Finchale, Godric built his cell of thatch, dedicating it to the Virgin Mary, where he lived 63 years, in that heate of devotion that he would stand whole winter nights praying up to the neck in the river that ran by his cell; which so angered the devil that one time he stol away his clothes that lay on the bankside; but spying him, he brought him back with a *Pater* and *Ave Maria*, and, forcing the devil to be just against his will, made them restore them, though his apparel was soe coarse that the devil (the thief) would scarce have worn them; for his jerkin was of iron, of which he had worn out three in the tyme of his hermitage; a strange coat, whos stuffe had the ironmonger for the draper, and a smith for the taylour. Neither was his lodging softer than his coat, who had a stone for his pillow, and the ground for his bed; but his diet was as coarse as either; for to repent both within and without, as his shirt was of sackcloth, soe half the meal that made him bread was ashes. An angel sometimes played the sexton and rang his bell to awaken him to his Nocturnes, who, for want of beads, used to number his prayers with pebble stons. The devil, Proteus-like, used to transforme himself into shapes before him, which rather made him sport than affrighted him, which so provoked the devil that, as he sate by his fyre, he gave Godrick such a boxe on the ear, that had he not recovered himselfe with the sign of the crosse he had feld him downe. He had the psalter continually handing on his little finger, which with use was ever crooked. Thus, after he had acted all the miracles of a legend, he ended his scene in the year 1170.

Robert Hegg, *The Legend of St Cuthbert* (1626)

An engraving of the medieval buildings at Finchale Priory. This was where Godric (d. 1170) set up his hermitage and where his holiness and prophetic gifts attracted visitors. After his death his shrine was greatly visited by women seeking medical cures, 1835.

Hobthrush Island, Lindisfarne, used by Aidan and Cuthbert and reputedly where Cuthbert dispelled a devil. (Photo: Geoff Doel)

After the saint's death (he was never officially declared a saint, but was locally thought to be one), his hermitage and its site was granted by Bishop Flambard to the monastery of Durham to be 'inhabited by such brethren as they might appoint'. A church and cloistral buildings were built and Godric's shrine became a popular place of pilgrimage much visited particularly by local women seeking medical cures – over 200 miracles were recorded. There was an on-site guest house for pilgrims and Godric is known to have contacted several pilgrims in their dreams.

To one pilgrim he let it be known that he objected to the stench of the public latrines which had been situated by the church in which he was enshrined.

Another pilgrim said he saw the saint in his dream lift his coffin lid to get in and out.

The Hobthrush Hermits

Aidan and Cuthbert both spent time as hermits on this tiny island off the coast of Lindisfarne, the *Denham Tracts* mentions that the island was named after a spirit who haunted it, and that it was expelled by St Cuthbert.

Inner Farne where Aidan, Cuthbert and Bartholomew and others set up their hermitages. (Photo: Geoff Doel)

St Cuthbert's Chapel, Inner Farne where Bartholomew set up his stone coffin. (Photo: Geoff Doel)

Hermits of Inner Farne

The three great saints who famously used the island as a hermitage were Aidan, Cuthbert and Bartholomew, though other monks from the motherhouse at Durham also spent time there. Aidan miraculously saved Bamburgh from destruction while on retreat on Inner Farne. Penda and his Mercian army had attacked the royal fortress and piled up combustibles against the city walls intending to burn it down. Bede tells us that when the saint on his island saw the column of smoke rising above Bamburgh:

> … he raised his eyes and hands to heaven saying: 'Lord, see what the evil Penda does!' No sooner were the words out of his mouth when the wind shifted from the city and drove the flames back on to those who had kindled them, so injuring some and unnerving all that they abandoned their assault on the city so clearly under God's protection.

During Cuthbert's eleven-year stay on the island as its hermit, he expelled evil spirits that haunted the island, moved great stones in order to build his hermitage with the help of angel hands, magically produced a spring of pure water to serve his needs from dry ground, and obtained a crop from seed sown out of season.

Bartholomew gained fame with the austerity of his religious practices, but could not get on with his fellow hermits who objected to Bartholomew's smelly hair shirt which he never ever removed and whose smell sickened the first hermit. The second hermit was an ex-prior: 'The two settled on the same spot and regarded each other with jealousy and dislike – and anything but a saint-like spirit was manifested'. After spending forty-two years on Farne Bartholomew was overcome with the weakness of old age and was buried in a stone coffin which he had cut for himself with own hands on the south side of St Cuthbert's chapel.

The Warkworth Hermits

A fourteenth-century stone hermitage, which was lived in by a number of hermit cum chantry priests, was created by the Lords of Warkworth expressly to pray for the souls of the dead Percy family. It consists of a tiny chapel hollowed out in the sandstone cliff overlooking the River Coquet near the castle, with a tiny adjacent room with an altar, possibly an oratory, and a living room with a fireplace. The hermit incumbent was permitted to farm the lands above the hermitage, keep cows and a servant, and in addition to a stipend he received a basket of fish and logs for his fire.

The best known hermit story is the legendary tale of two young lovers from the Percy ballad *The Hermit of Warkworth*. Sir Bertram, a young knight and vassal of Lord Percy, loves Lady Isabel, daughter of the Lord of Widdrington. Seeking to test his love, Isabel presents her courtly lover with 'a plumed casque with golden crest' which must be 'dinted with many a foeman's blows' before she will consent to be his. Lord Percy was just then being harassed by the Douglases who were wreaking havoc in the borderlands and carrying off the Percy flocks. When the two forces clash on open moorland, Bertram, inspired by his love for Isabel, mows down his foes 'like poppies in a field', but falls when a 'giant

Warkworth Hermitage where the hermits of Warkworth Castle were employed to pray for the souls of the Percy family. (Photo: Geoff Doel)

An interior view of Warkworth Hermitage. (Photo: Geoff Doel)

Warkworth Castle. (From Sir Walter Scott's *Marmion*, 1855 edition)

Douglas hand' delivers a blow which slices through his helmet to the brain. Bertram is carried from the bloody scene on a shield. He later recovers from his dreadful wounds, only to learn that the fair Isabel has been abducted by the Scots and has been taken over the border. The wretched young man adopts a series of disguises as he wanders over the Scottish borderlands searching for his lady until at last he comes across a lonely castle. In the dim morning light he sees his lady climbing down the castle wall on a silken ladder and awaiting her is a knight on horseback. They ride off together but Bertram pursues them, and engages the unknown knight in furious combat. When the knight falls dead, lady Isabel, wounded and dying herself, manages to inform Bertram (in eight stanzas) that she has ever been true to him and that he has slain his own brother:

> 'Bertram,' she said, 'be comforted,
> And live to think on me;
> May we in heaven that union prove
> Which here was not to be.'

There is no comfort for the young lord. He becomes a penitential hermit 'and the good Lord Percy provides a quiet hermitage by the River Coquet where he might pass his time in prayer until released by sweet death.'

The Gateshead Anchorite

In 1340 a license was granted by Bishop Bury:

> ... for the selecting and assigning of a fit space in the cemetery of the Church of the Blessed Mary ... contiguous to the church itself, to build on the same for the residence and habitation of a certain female anchoret, to be shut up therein, provided the good will and consent of the rector and parishioners should be given to the same.

St Mary's Island, where a hermit from Tynemouth Priory was thought to have been installed in the early twelfth century. (Photo: Geoff Doel)

The Hermit of Old Tyne Bridge

When the old Tyne Bridge was dismantled at the end of the eighteenth century after the great flood, one of the pillars of the bridge was found to be an anchorite cell in which the last incumbent had been buried. There is written evidence from a will that he had been 'enjoined to pray for the soul of Newcastle worthy the [celebrated] old Roger Thornton' who also founded the *Maison Dieu* or Hospital of St Katherine for nine poor men and four poor women, and provided them with meat and clothing in 1412. The anchorite was just one of thirty priests enjoined to sing for his soul.

The Hermit of St Mary's Island

It is thought that one of monks of Tynemouth Priory took up residence here as a hermit at precisely the same time as Henry the Dane from Tynemouth Priory withdrew as a hermit to Coquet Island. A little chapel or chantry belonging to the Priory of Tynemouth and dedicated to St Mary was founded on St Mary's at an early period, 'but every trace of it has long disappeared. The only guide to its site is the inlet in the rocks known as St Mary's Bay, to which fishermen still run for shelter when caught in a storm'. According to tradition, a lamp was kept burning in the sanctuary during the night for the benefit of passing ships. In the tower was a bell, which was rung to summon aid in the event of a shipwreck on the coast. Attached to the chapel was a cemetery in which it was customary to bury the bodies of drowned sailors.

EIGHT

Gazetteer of Holy Wells

There are a number of wells and springs in the North which have for centuries been traditionally regarded as holy and regularly visited for their perceived curative properties. Some of these wells carry the names of saints and may have been linked to early Christian cells or primitive churches. In the Victorian period, the famous Romano-British Temple of Coventina on Hadrian's Wall was excavated. It had an enclosed sacred well from which was collected 16,000 coins made as offerings, as well as jewellery and ritual artefacts, indications of an important pre-Christian water cult.

The Christianised wells in Northumbria also yield votive offerings in the form of pins, often bent, or colourful rags tied to the branches of nearby trees or bushes. These are the 'Clooties' wells (cloot being a cloth or rag) and examples of this kind of hallowed well are found in Scotland, Cornwall, and Ireland. Writing in the nineteenth century, one folklorist researching holy wells in the North observed that 'not all holy wells are quite so old and it is believed that the traditions associated with some of the best known are of fairly recent origin', while another collector noted that 'most wells are springs but occasionally other water sources such as hollowed stones which collect water, are treated as holy wells'.

Peter B.G. Binnall, while researching Holy Wells in Northumberland and Durham, identified ninety-eight names of places in Northumberland where there were one or more holy wells, and twenty-five place names in Durham. The great majority of these 'holy wells' have long since disappeared. Binnall was convinced that the wells were frequented for healing and wish-fulfilment, 'but of all the therapeutic qualities commonly ascribed to holy wells', he noted, 'that of "healing sore eyes" was by far the commonest and most widely distributed.' He had also noted how in Northumberland there was 'evidence of a number of Midsummer traditions concerning holy wells' and suggested that after the change of calendar in 1752 some of these customs had slipped back into July, 'often on Midsummer Day Old Style – July 4th'.

This is a compilation of some of twenty-eight of the better known wells taken from a variety of sources as indicated in the text.

Hadrian's Wall, the site of the earliest holy pre-Christian well, Coventina's Well is by the fort of Brocolitia. (From Sir Walter Scott's *Guy Mannering*)

Akeld
Denham calls it a 'Medieval chapel and Wishing Well' and adds, 'drink and wish but no known offering'.

Allendale Town
A chalybeate spring situated on the brow of the hill 'the waters of which are considered to be efficacious in cleansing the blood'.

Allen Heads
In the nineteenth century it was claimed to be 'a medicinal spring used for scorbutics and gravel'.

Alnham
St Andrew's Wells.

Alnwick
The Freman's Well. As described by Denham in 1851, 'The singular and filthy custom of leaping the well on St Mark's Day at Alnwick, fell into almost total disuse this year, and it is almost more than probable that the year 1852 will see the usage entirely abandoned. Peace to its ashes!'

The Pin Well in Hulne Park was a wishing well. 'To ensure the fulfilment of a wish, walk three times round the well, jump across, throw in a pin, and wish.' It was not thought to be medicinal.

The Senna Well near Alnwick was thought to be medicinal but debatably not because it had the virtue of senna pods!

Alwinton
A cryptic foot note from *Archaeologia Aeliana*, viii, says 'Holystone, Lady's Well, near Alwinton. Railed in pool Here Paulinus said to have baptised 3,000 persons Easter 627 but no evidence. Missionaries may have preached at the Holy Stone … Dr Embleton informs me he has formerly noticed many pins lying in the bottom.'

Bellingham
Cuddy's Well (i.e. St Cuthbert's Well). The well is situated outside the church wall. It is reputed to be a healing well and is credited with many miracles.

Benton
The Rag Well is where votaries once left fragments of garments on the trees and bushes.

Bingfield
Bourne gives a description of the Bore Well (a sulphur well) rituals on Erring Bridge:

> On the Sunday following the 4th day of July that is about Midsummer Day according to the old style, a great crowd of people used to assemble here from all surrounding hamlets and villages. The scene has been described to me as resembling a fair, stalls for the sale of various refreshments being brought from a distance year by year at the summer solstice. The neighbouring slopes had been terraced, and seats formed for the convenience of pilgrims and visitors. One special object of female pilgrims was, I am informed, to pray at the well, or express a silent wish as they stood over it for the cure of barrenness. The festival was called 'Bore Well Sunday'.

Birtley
A description of the rituals enacted at the well are given in *Archaeologia Aeliana*, viii: 'There the villager of a generation ago frequented the well in the early hours of the New Year … they held that the fortunate first visitant of the well who should fill his flask or bottle with the water … brought good luck to the house in which it remained.'

Colwell
From the *Proceeding of the Society of Antiquaries of Newcastle upon Tyne*, iv: 'The annual festival was held on or about the 4th of July (St Ulric's Day), and consisted of a popular pilgrimage to the well at Colwell, and dressing it with flowers. This "Bridal of Colwell" is no longer remembered.'

Gilsland

From *Archaeologia Aeliana*, vii: 'Within my own recollection, the yearly pilgrimage to Gilsland wells on the Sunday after old Midsummer Day, is called the Head Sunday, and the Sunday after it, was a very remarkable survival of the ancient cultus of primitive times.'

Hartley

From the *Proceedings of the Society of Antiquaries of Newcastle-upon-Tyne*, v, 1882: 'If the visitor cares to look into the holy well itself he will see innumerable crooked pins, which have been cast in by the faithful of the present day.'

Hedgehope

From *County Folk Lore*:

On the top of 'Hedgehope', the round headed hill that is neighbour to Cheviot, there is a hollow in an incised stone, known as the 'Bloody Trough' on account of the colour given to the water by the orange moss or lichen covering the stone. It is lucky to make a wish here, and drop in a crooked pin – a great number can be seen clearly, lying at the bottom of the hollow, in the water.

Horsdean

The Pin Well. From James Hall's *A Guide to Glendale* (1887): 'On May Day a procession was formed and marched from the town to this spot, where a halt was called and each of the processionists dropped a crooked pin into it, at the same time wishing a wish.'

Jesmond

Our Lady's Well. From Richardson, *The Borderer's Table Book*:

The Holy Well and shrine at this place were anciently in high estimation, and resorted to by pilgrims, who came from all parts of the kingdom to worship there. It has a reputation as a healing well. The well was enclosed by William Coulson, Esq., who purchased possession here in 1669 [as] a bathing place, which was no sooner done than the water left it. This was considered a just revenge for profaning the sacred well; but the water soon returned and the miracle was ended.

Jarrow

Bede's Well. Brand comments in his *Observations on Popular Antiquities, chiefly illustrating the origin of our vulgar Customs, Ceremonies, and Superstitions* that:

As late as 1740 it was a prevailing custom to bring children troubled with any infirmity; a crooked pin was put in, and the well laved dry between each dipping. Twenty children were brought together on a Sunday to be dipped in this well, and at Midsummer Eve there was a great resort by neighbouring people. This concourse at the summer solstice was attended with bonfires, music, dancing, and other rural sports, but customs discontinued before 1812.

Keyheugh

A pin well in the parish of Elsdon, Northumberland.

Lambton

From the *Denham Tracts*:

The 'Worm Well' co Durham had formerly a cover and an iron ladle. Half a century ago (i.e. 1800) it was in repute as a wishing well, and was one of the scenes dedicated to the usual festivities and superstitions of Midsummer Eve. A crooked pin may sometimes still be discovered sparkling amongst the clear gravel of the bottom of its basin.

Longwitton

From Hodgson, *History of Northumberland* part I, vol. iii:

A little to the east of them (Longwitton Hall Gardens), in a wood, are three wells, which rise beneath a thick stratum of sandstone rock which the people of the neighbourhood call *Our Lady's Wells* and *The Holy Wells*. They are all chalybeate, contain sulphur and alumina, and were formerly in high reputation through the neighbourhood for their 'very virtuous' qualities. That farthest to the east is called *Eyewell,* on account of its beneficial effects in cases of inflammation of the eyes and flux of the lachrymal humour … Great concourses of people from all parts … used to assemble here … on 'Midsummer Sunday and the Sunday following' and amuse themselves with leaping, eating gingerbread brought for sale to the spot, and drinking the waters of the wells.

Otterburn

From Murray's *Handbook to Durham and Northumberland* part II: 'Another spring is called *The Wishing Well* from the local belief that every wish made there is sure to be granted.'

Seaham

Lady Byron's Well. From Apperley, *Folk-Lore of the County of Durham* (1910): 'Pins may sometimes be seen in Lady Byron's Well.'

Wark

From *Archaeologia Aeliana*, viii:

There are three wells, Old Kirk, High Well, Riverside Well. On New Year's Morning within memory, each of these wells was visited by the villagers in the hope of their being the first to take what was called the 'Flower of the Well'. Whoever first drank of the spring would obtain, it was believed, marvellous powers throughout the next year, even to the extent of being able to pass through keyholes and take nocturnal flights in the air. The fortunate recipient of such extraordinary power notified his or her acquisition thereof by casting into the well an offering of flowers or grass, hay or straw, from seeing which the next earliest devotees would know that their labour was in vain.

Wooler Magic Wells
From the *Monthly Chronicle*, 1888:

The Fairy Wishing, Maiden or Pin Well, Wooler. A curious custom here associated with May. On May Day a procession was formed and marched from the town to this spot, a halt called and each processional dropped a crooked pin into it, at the same time 'wishing a wish' in the fond belief, that before the year was over the fairy or genius who presided over the well, would cause the wish to be realised. Though the procession at May Day is longer enacted the superstition regarding it has not entirely disappeared. Thither youngsters go and drop in their pins. Overhead is the King's chair. According to tradition a certain king sat and directed the order of battle which was fought in the ravine.

Wooler
From the *Daily Journal*, 'North Country Notes,' 26 January 1893:

There is at Wooler a well, where, according to an ancient custom lovers go at midnight, and after bending and throwing into the water a pin, they wish for a speedy marriage or some other lover-like wish, which, according to the villagers, is bound to come true. Judging from the number of bent pins lying at the bottom, I should imagine there are still a host of believers in the old custom.

NINE

WITCHES OF THE NORTH

In the 'enlightened' eighteenth century fear of witches and their powers entirely ceased to be an issue in Northumberland and Durham, as elsewhere in England.

Before that, however, there had been a long period, starting with the last years of Elizabeth I and particularly during the years of the Commonwealth, in which the men and women of the English North and at all levels of society were deeply disturbed by stories that just over the border the Scottish Kirk accepted that not only did witches exist, but that they derived supernatural powers from the Devil. Manically anti-superstition and fiercely anti-Catholic, the Kirk began systematically to purge the land of men and women whom they claimed had manifested supernatural abilities through demonic means. It was maintained that witches worked through charms, spells, incantations and the evil eye to inflict sickness and death on neighbours and their beasts, they brought rain, storm and hail to damage crops and they could foresee the future. Condemnation was followed by arrest; arrest was followed by systematic torture and torture was followed by public burnings; the Bible attested 'you must not suffer a witch to live'.

Panic and fear inevitably seeped through to the northern areas and in 1650 Newcastle Council was petitioned to deal with witches within the city. The petition must have come from influential quarters for the council immediately sent over the border for a Scottish self-styled 'witch-finder' able to seek out the 'Children of the Devil'. The fee was set at 20s for each witch 'discovered and condemned'.

Once in the city, the Scottish procedure for discovering a witch was put in place. A town crier progressed throughout the walled city ringing his bell and ordering that any *woman* [our italics] suspected of being a witch should have her name handed in to the Town Hall. Thirty names were written down and the suspects were herded into the town hall before a fascinated crowd. One by one each woman was forced to expose her body below the waist while a long pin was pushed several times into her thighs or buttocks and left for a few seconds. The theory behind this was that a witch had 'insensible' flesh and would not bleed. The women were also asked if they could feel anything; not surprisingly, most were too shocked to say anything at all. The witch-finder did not rely on this test, claiming instead that he could recognise a witch on sight.

Not all the onlookers found the evidence convincing or impressive. One army man insisted that one of the accused be re-tried. This time the woman clearly bled when the pin was withdrawn and the town sergeants set her free. She was observed to be a well-dressed, respectable looking person. This might imply that the others were drawn from a poorer element of the population.

The unsurprising result of all this was that in August 1650 a gallows was set up on the Town Moor and sixteen townspeople (one man and fifteen women) were hanged in public.

> The 21 day of August thes partes her under named wer executed in the Town mor for wichvu, Isab' Brown, Margrit Muddeuon, Ann Watson, Ellenor Henderson, Ellenor Rogers, Elsabeth Dobson, Mathew Bonner or Boumer, Mrs Ellsabeth Anderson, Jane Hunter, Jane Koupling, Margrit Brown, Margrit Moffet …Karen Wellsh for a Wich, Aylles Hume, Marie Postes.

The Scotsman later claimed that he had been responsible for the deaths of 220 women; he had earned over £400.

There are two important nineteenth-century collections of Northumberland and Durham witchcraft activity in antiquity, William Weaver Tomlinson's *Life in Northumberland During the Sixteenth Century* and the *Denham Tracts*. Both draw on *Depositions and Other Ecclesiastical Proceedings from the Courts of Durham, Extending from 1311, to the Reigns of Elizabeth*, and *Depositions from the Castle of York, Relating to Offences Committed in the Northern Counties in the Seventeenth Century* later issued in two volumes by the Surtees Society in 1845 and 1861. There are so many cases of perceived witchcraft that we can only give a sample selection of the more salient characteristics.

In the late Elizabethan period, the easily procured 'riddle [sieve] and shears' were widely used for all sorts of trivial divinatory purposes – to predict love matters, find lost goods, forecast the weather etc. However, if you were known to have consulted a 'wise woman' or used them yourself to forecast some future event, there could be serious consequences for this was perceived as witchcraft and an offence against Church and State:

> … albeit it [i.e. divination] seam to some to be but a trifling matter, yet seing it as a kinde of divination or charming, expressly forbidden by Gode's laws and the Queen's Majestie, and cannot be done without a defection and mistrust to God and some confidence to the devell.

Between 1561 and 1577 one Alice Swan was brought before the authorities accused of divining (for a fee, and at the prompting of six local housewives). During the interrogation some leading questions were put to her and her answers written down by a clerk of the court. This 'confession' was later read out aloud by the minister in St Nicholas Church at Newcastle-upon-Tyne after the sermon, while Alice stood humbly penitent before the congregation. It was devised as a humiliation and punishment and a warning to all the good ladies present.

Here is Alice Swan's confession from the Surtees Society *Depositions and other Ecclesiastical Proceedings from the Courts of Durham* no. 21:

I, Alice Swan, by the means and procurement of Margaret Lawson, Anne Hedworth, Elizabeth Kindleside, Agnes Rikerby, Anne Bewike, and Jerrerd Robinson, not having the feare of God before myne eyes, but following the persuasion of the devil, who moveth me and all mankind to a defection from God our Creator, have of filthie lucre, and under colour of a singular and secret knowledge of lost thinges, used by the space of certen yeres to cast or tourney the riddle and sheares, and wherefore I am comen here this day … humbly to acknowledge and confesse my foresaid offence before you all …

Despite ecclesiastical and civic disapprobation, divination using riddle and shears and dozens of other forms of fortune-telling lingered well into the seventeenth century in the North.

Witchcraft trials and depositions in the North are often full of references to unexplained or protracted or painful illnesses because these were often attributed to witchcraft. It was often claimed a witch had 'overlooked' a victim, causing them to languish or waste away. The *Denham Tracts* gives an example of this:

Frances Mason, daughter of a soldier at Tynemouth, Feb. 15, 1659-60, having lost the power of her limbs, attributes it to one Elizabeth Simpson, who she said tormented her in her bed, 'and did pinch her heart and pull her in pieces': whereupon the father drew blood from the accused, and his daughter obtained quiet, but not the use of her limbs.

Elizabeth Simpson's trial mentions that the aggrieved father, Michael Mason, 'drew blood' from the 'witch'. This was regularly done in the case of suspected witchcraft where people felt threatened; magistrates rarely reprimanded anyone for taking the law into their own hands for this, even when disfigurement followed. 'Drawing blood' also known as 'scoring above the breath' was done by making cuts on the witch's forehead or cheeks often in the form of a cross – and it was usual to use a knife, pin or nail. The belief was that this disempowered the witch.

Part of the power of a witch lay in her ability to shape-shift – to change into a hare, cat, mouse or whatever. This was regularly claimed and believed in the seventeenth century even though while in prison and under interrogation no witch was ever observed to shape-shift or managed to escape in the form of a beetle, mouse or rat. Note in the following example that Jane Milburne underplays the fact that she has 'scored' her aunt.

In 1664, Dorothy Stranger was brought to trial accused by her niece Jane Milburne, wife of William Milburne of Newcastle-upon-Tyne of being a witch. Jane claimed that she had been verbally abused and threatened by her aunt, Dorothy Stranger, after omitting to invite her to a family wedding. Soon after this family quarrel Dorothy appeared to Jane in 'the perfect similitude of a cat':

And the said catt did leape at her face and did vocally speake with a very audible voice, and said that itt had gotten the life of on in the howse and came for this informer life, and would have it before Saturday night. To which she replyed 'I defye the, the devil, and all his works.' Upon which the catt did vanish. And upon Saturday last, aboute 8 of the clocke in the morning, she goeing down to the seller for to draw a quart of beare, and opening the seller doore, which was locked, she visibly did see the said Dorothy Strange standing in the seller, leaneing with her armes upon one of ht hodgheads, and said then to this informer, 'Theafe, art thow there yett? Thy life I seeke, thy lyfe I will have' … Upon Sunday last, about one of the clocke, this informer putting on her clothes in her chamber to goe to church, there did appear to her a catt of the same shape as the former, and did leap at her throat … And the said catt did bit her arme and did hold itt very fast, and made a great impression in her arme with her teth and did lett her hold goe and disappeared. And yesterday in the afternoone, about tow of the clock, this informer comeing down the stares, the said catt did violently leape about her neck and shoulder, and was so ponderous that she was not able to support itt, but did bring her downe to the ground and kept her downe for the space of a quarter of an houre. And she was soe infirme and disenabled that the power of both body and tongue were taken from her … And this informant verily beleives that the said catt which appeared to her was Dorothy Stranger, and non else. And she, having a desire to see her did this morning send for the said Dorothy, butt she was very loth to come, and comeing to her she gott blood of her at the said Stranger's desire, and since hath been pritye well.

Did the magistrates ask the right questions? Did they find the claims of witchcraft offered by Jane Milburne rational, sensible and well supported by the evidence? Or did these educated, socially superior, good Protestants and pillars of the community, find the evidence quite consistent with their own belief in the amazing ability of these very ordinary women to magically transpose themselves into animal form and through *maleficia* (personal spite) harm good Christian members of society? If Dorothy was found guilty she would have been hanged.

Some witches were known as 'white witches' and variously termed as 'wise man', 'conjuror' or 'wise woman'; they often offered their services in the community either for money or gifts and their services were extremely varied. Some had ways of looking into the future using divinatory objects; many could provide preventative magic in the form of counter-spells, charms and potions to ward off perceived evil. Others were termed 'medicers' because of their knowledge of herbal medicine and their acknowledged gifts as healers for men and beasts.

An example of a northern 'medicer' appears in the parish register of Hart Church, County Durham for 28 July 1582. Two women, Janet Allenson and Janet Bainbridge of Stockton, had consulted Allison Lawe 'for the cure of the sick'. Allison was reported to the authorities, taken into custody, and was lucky to get off lightly. She was written up as 'a notorious sorcerer and enchanter' and her punishment was public humiliation and to do public penance. She was obliged to stand (presumably all day) 'with a papir on her head' (declaring her a witch?) – once in the market-place at Durham, once in Hart Church, and once in Norton Church.

At this time few in a community could afford doctors, and though most housewives had their own simples or herbal recipes, many appeared to have called regularly on the services of women like Allison in the community with a flair or reputation for medical knowledge. Part of the problem appears to have been that the 'medicers' tended to employ charms or to engage in superstitious rituals which were viewed by an ultra-Protestant element in the community as smacking of popery or devilry. This was very apparent in the case of one Mistress Pepper, a Newcastle midwife, who was reported to the authorities for using superstitious curative rituals which involved holy water and a silver crucifix which she carried about in her bag.

From the Visitation Book, Register Office, Durham, in the early seventeenth century, the Vicar General of the Bishop of Durham proceeded against Katharine Thompson and Anne Nevelson of Wooler 'for being common charmers of sick folks and their goods, and that they use[d] to bring white ducks or drakes to set the bill thereof to the mouth of the sick person, and mumble up their charms in such strange manner as is damnable and horrible'.

L'Estrange Ewen derides what must be one of the most bizarre cases of witchcraft in the North – that of the servant Annie Armstrong. In 1673 Annie came before no less than three magistrates and each time because of her evidence people in her community were imprisoned and interrogated. One of Annie's 'stories' was that she had taken part in a 'covey' of witches along with the devil, and that as part of the activities the witches swung wildly on a bell rope during which time they magically obtained food and drink. Ewen sees her as a hysteric and 'not worthy of credence'.

Reporting a witch to the authorities and having the assizes deal with them was just one way of dealing with unpopular people who were rumoured to be witches. The common people had their own way of coping with witch activity in the community as noted by Denham: You could, for example, nail a horse shoe 'upwards upon the door or threshold of the byre, stable or dwelling-house … [for it] hinders the power of witches'. Denham also informs us that in the recent past (the eighteenth century) country people used to wear a little bone as an amulet round the neck to protect them from witches. The bone was taken from a sheep's head and was chosen because it had the shape of a T [Tau or cross] and was considered a sacred and protective symbol. Other talismans were sprigs of rowan, holed stones or a bunch of ash keys to keep them safe from a witch's powers. Housewives baking bread each morning performed …

> … a useful and necessary ceremony, the moment they lay the leaven-trough, containing the batch of dough, down upon the hearthstone to rise previous to its baking. The process is simple, and is performed by making the sign of the cross thereon with the forefinger of the right hand; and this act not only prevents the dough from sticking to the pasteboard, but also from falling; as it is termed both before and after putting it into the oven and … also prevents witches exercising any of their devilish arts in connection herewith.

It was also commonly believed that running water kept away witches.

The Oral Tales

There are a few oral tales on witchcraft exclusive to Northumberland and Durham, which, although recorded at a very late period, may help reconstruct popular beliefs in the North surrounding local witchcraft at an earlier period.

The first tale, 'The Easington Hare' reflects the commonly held folk belief that witches were shape-shifters. The animal most often selected was the hare, possibly because of its staying power and speed. The tale gives us insights into a primitive rural society given to consulting 'conjurors' (male witches); these men because of their herbal knowledge, were often the 'doctors' and vets of an area, but they also had expertise in forecasting the weather (important in agrarian societies) and dabbled in magic, particularly charms and spells; they were also consulted because of their ability to 'scry' (look into the past and future). We are also given the stereotype of a female witch – the isolated, illiterate, impoverished, unhappy old woman living alone in a cottage; surviving records of sixteenth- and seventeenth-century witch trials in the North indicate that while not all witches conformed to this type, social misfits and the mentally ill, and particularly those of straightened means or of a lower social order were those most often picked upon by their more fortunate neighbours to be denounced to the authorities as witches.

The Story of the Easington Hare

At one time the men of Castle Eden bred greyhounds, which they trained to take part in hare coursing. But their hunting days were effectively brought to an end when a large dark-coloured hare appeared on the scene. The greyhounds went mad when they saw it and pursued it all over the country. They ignored their masters' whistles to desist. Many ran to their death. Others ran clean out of the county and were never seen again. The Castle Eden men took advice from a local conjuror, a wise man who knew how to heal sick horses and cows. They were told to go out with a coal-black bloodhound – one that was fed on human milk. The hare was soon found and driven out by the hound into the open countryside pursued by the huntsmen on horseback. As they were passing by the village of Easington the hare veered in its path and disappeared into a cottage, though the bloodhound managed to bite its leg just before it disappeared. The huntsmen broke their way into the cottage for no one answered the door when they knocked. Inside they found an exhausted old woman with a bloody leg. The hare never appeared again in the locality.

The very reporting of a neighbour's name as a witch to the authorities would have occasioned arrest and imprisonment. Many women were known to have been physically abused while in custody. Others, sometimes waiting months in primitive and unwholesome prison conditions before the Assizes, must have deteriorated physically and mentally; many died.

This second oral tale on the Wallsend Witches comes from the *Folklore* series. It seems to reflect some of the 'new' ideas about witchcraft which James I had introduced into English law when he became King of England in the early seventeenth century. James, influenced by continental ideas, became entirely persuaded that witches drew their power from the Devil with whom they had made a covenant, organised themselves into covens and met together in desecrated churches. James personally attended witch trials and interrogations: an intelligent man, he appears to have quickly come to the conclusion that liars and malicious neighbours had as much to do with witchcraft as the beliefs about the powers of witches.

The hag-like witches of Wallsend in this story may have been influenced by Shakespeare's *Macbeth* though their cannibalism adds a gothic *frisson* to the tale. The drowning of the Wallsend witch in the Coquet runs contrary to the older belief that witches could not drown but could only float in water, while the death of a witch by burning did not happen in England and suggests either a borrowing or sensationalism.

The Story of the Wallsend Witches

One dark evening, the young lord of Seaton Delaval was riding past a ruined chapel in Wallsend when he observed bright lights within and heard strange muttering noises. He crept up to the west door and peered in. Inside he could see the altar on which were the body parts of a human female body; an old hag was butting off the breast. Twelve other witches were gathered in the nave centred round a blazing fire (made from chopped up pews). They were selecting objects from a sack and dropping them into a bubbling cauldron. As each object fell into the vessel each witch in turn cast a malevolent spell designed to blight crops and to do harm to beast and men. Enraged, the young lord burst through the door and fell upon the chief witch; he dragged her outside and rode off with her to his great house at Seaton Delavel. Here she was kept in confinement until her trial; she was sentenced to death by burning on the seashore by the vicinity of Seaton Delavel for her misdeeds.

As the locals gathered round her pyre, the witch was granted a last request. She requested 'two little wooden dishes that have never held water'. As soon as these items were laid at her feet she jumped upon them whereupon she was lifted up into the air; soon she was circling above the crowd's heads jeering and cursing. But her magical escape was foiled because one of the dishes was not new. When it fell from her foot she dropped like a stone. Some say she drowned in the river and others that she was taken still alive to the shore line and burned.

Today we are all well acquainted with the idea of friendly wizards, thanks to the Harry Potter books and films. The third Northumbrian oral tale deals with a highly educated, and sophisticated practitioner of magic who lived in the thirteenth century and was once well known in the North. His name was Michael Scott, sometimes known as Duns Scotis, and it is claimed that he once cast a spell to help the good people of Morpeth. An account of some of his other spells appears in Sir Walter Scott's poem 'The Lay of the Last Minstrel' (1805), which illustrates 'the customs and manners which anciently prevailed on the Borders of England and Scotland' and is put into the mouth of a sixteenth-century minstrel:

It was my lot
To meet the wonderous Michael Scott;
A wizard of such dreaded fame,
That when, in Salamanca's cave,
Him listed his magic wand to wave,
The bells would ring in Notre Dame
Some of his skills he taught to me;
And, warrior, I could say to thee
The words that cleft Eildon hills in three,
And bridled the Tweed with a curb of stone:
But to speak them were a deadly sin.

According to Walter Scott's notes on this poem, Michael Scott (*c.* 1175–*c.* 1234) was born in Balwearie though there are other traditions that he may have been born or brought up in the north-east of England (Durham is suggested) though of Scottish parentage. Certainly in the popular mind Duns Scotis was a wizard even if in his day he was well respected by scholars throughout Europe as a philosopher. He is believed to have been educated at the universities of Oxford and Paris and afterwards worked in some of the great courts of Europe. His academic fame rests on his scholarly works which were written in Latin and his translations of certain Arabic and Hebrew texts. Sir Walter Scott informs us that 'He appears to have been addicted to the abstruse studies of judicial astrology, alchemy, physiognomy, and chiromancy. Hence he passed among his contemporaries for a skilful magician'. Here is the Northumbrian oral tale as it appears in a late nineteenth-century form.

The Story of Michael Scott & the People of Morpeth

On one occasion the great magician Michael Scott was passing through Morpeth and was asked by the townspeople to turn the landlocked town into a seaport through magic. The wizard, who had already used magic spirits to help him construct a dam over the River Tweed at Kelso and to split the Eildon Hill in three, did not think the task impossible and asked that the finest runner in town be brought before him. A fine strong young man who could run like a deer was produced and the wizard ordered him to go to the seashore 'where the River Wansbeck meets the sea' and to wait on the shore until high tide. 'Then', he said, 'you begin your run to Morpeth. The waters will rush behind you, but never, ever, at any point, look behind you'. The young man agreed and the following day began his run as ordered. But things did not go well for the young runner for he had not known that the waves would bank into a great high wall of water, and was charged full of malicious screaming spirits. On and on he went, mile after mile, until he had passed the little village of Bothal and knew that he was nearing home. But now he was exhausted and the screams were louder and more threatening. Suddenly afraid, the runner looked behind him. In a second the great wave with its banshee spirits disappeared; the spell had broken.

Thus the burgess of Morpeth lost the chance of having the Wansbeck navigable between their town and the sea. It is also said that Michael intended to confer a similar favour on the inhabitants of Durham by making the Wear navigable to their city; but his good intentions, which were to be carried into effect in the same manner, were also frustrated through the cowardice of the person who had to 'guide the tide'.

TEN

THE TURNING YEAR: SEASONAL CUSTOMS & RITUALS

The agricultural cycle and the Church's formal and established ritual practices, especially liturgical procedure, determined the cyclic rhythm of the year and included the major festivals of Christmas and Easter, Corpus Christi with its great processions of clergy and laity, the Marian Festivals, All Souls' (later to become Halloween) and numerous celebrations of saints' days. By the order of Henry VIII certain of the Catholic feast days (such as days devoted to the Virgin Mary, the Holy Cross and Corpus Christi) were removed from the Church calendar. The Church of England continued to maintain the yearly round of Christian feasts and festivals and these, until fairly recently, played a vitally important role in village life.

The *Denham Tracts* list the traditional foodstuffs associated with the major festivals in the nineteenth century – a turkey and mince-pie at Christmas; a gammon of bacon on Easter Day; a goose on Michaelmas day; oysters on St James's Day; a roast pig on St Bartlemy's Day; a fat hen at Shrovetide; ham or bacon collops on Shrove Monday; pancakes on Shrove Tuesday; a male pullet and bacon on Fasten Day, hot cross buns on Good Friday; bull beef at Candlemass; eggs on the Saturday before Shrove Tuesday, salmon and all kinds of fish in Lent.

Bede tells us that the heathen Saxon year began on 25 September which was called 'Mothers' Night' and that the December–January period was called Giuli (Yule).

St Nicholas' Eve, 5 December: Boy Bishop

An ancient Christian concession to the Roman Saturnalian practice of inversion of the natural order of things at specific times in midwinter is the election of a choirboy as Boy Bishop to preach a service. Due to the link between St Nicholas and children, this was often done on St Nicholas' Eve or Day. Denham comments:

It was generally practised about the period of St Nicholas's day (6th December), who, it may be proper to remark, was the chosen patron of schoolboys. On this day was formerly celebrated the semi-impious … farce of the Boy Bishop, one of whom, in the year 1229, was permitted to say vespers before King Edward I, at the Chapel of Heton, near Newcastle-on-Tyne; and the king was so much pleased with his youthful chaplain and choral followers that he made them a considerable present.

Some seventy or eighty years ago vestiges of these medieval, at least, if not primeval, customs were retained in several of the grammar schools of the whole of the north of England. Brand says that he heard the custom was retained in the Dean and Chapter's schools in the city of Durham, and that the same practice prevailed in the Kepier School, of Houghton-le-Spring, in the county of Durham. It prevailed also at Rothbury in Northumberland.

Christmas

Nineteenth-century accounts of Christmas celebrations in Northumbria indicate that houses were decorated with greenery – holly, mistletoe, ivy and yew – and that these were taken down on Twelfth Night. It was a Durham tradition that evergreens should not be burnt:

> If you burn green
> Your sorrow's soon seen.

In the early nineteenth century the *Denham Tracts* record a 'Kissing Bush' at Newcastle-upon-Tyne, formed of mistletoe, evergreens, ribbons and oranges. Garlands made with hoops covered in coloured paper and decorated with toys were recorded in mining villages in Durham.

The Yule Log or Yule Clog was laid on the fire on Christmas Eve, and if possible kept burning all the following day or longer. A portion of the log was kept to light up the new log the following Christmas, and to preserve the family from harm during the intervening year. Mrs Balfour noted that:

> In Belford the lord of the manor sends round to every house, on the afternoon of Christmas Eve, the Yule Logs – four or five large logs – to be burnt on Christmas Eve and Day. This old custom has always, I am told, been kept up here.

Traditional Christmas food included haggis for breakfast – 'made sometimes of fruit, suet, and minced entrails, and sometimes only of oatmeal, suet, and sugar, stuffed into a sheep's maw and boiled' – 'Yule dollies' or 'Yulie doos' made from dough or pastry or gingerbread with crossed arms and currants for eyes and buttons. There was 'general feasting' on currant dumplings, 'to cook which most of the kail (cabbage) pots were put'. In Durham, frumenty (wheat boiled in milk) was eaten.

The *Denham Tracts* list further practices:

To send a Vessle-cup [Wassail-cup] Singer away from your doors unrequited (at least the first that comes) is to forfeit the good luck of all the approaching year. Every family that can possibly afford it at least have a Yule cheese and Yule cake provided against Christmas Eve, and it is considered very unlucky to cut either of them before that festival of all festivals. A tall mould candle, called a Yule candle, is lighted in the evening and set upon the table, these candles are presented by the chandlers and grocers to their customers. The Yule Log is either bought of the carpenter's apprentice or found in some neighbour's field. It would be unlucky to light either the log or candle till the proper period; so also it is considered unlucky to stir the fire or move the candlestick during the supper, neither must the candle be snuffed, nor any one stir from the table till supper is ended. In these suppers it is considered unlucky to have an odd number at table, especially so if thirteen … A fragment of the log is occasionally saved and put under a bed to remain till next Christmas, it secures the house from fire, and a small piece of it thrown into a fire (occurring at the house of a neighbour) will quell the raging element. A piece of the candle should be kept to ensure good luck. No person, except boys, must presume to go out of doors till the threshold has been consecrated by the footsteps of a male. The entrance of a woman on the morning of this day, as well as on that of the New Year, is considered as the height of ill-luck. St Stephen's day in the north is devoted pretty generally to hunting and shooting, the game laws being considered as not in force on that day.

Mummers Plays

The general absence of Christmas and New Year Mummers Plays on the east coast is one of life's mysteries and generally the sword-dance functions as a seasonal alternative, often with a play with its own death and resurrection symbolism. The *Denham Tracts* does, however, cite some Guisarding Rhymes, which seem to be an abbreviated play with two alternative beginnings featuring a distinctive Goliath hero:

Redd room, redd room, for Guisard's sport,
For to this house I must resort;
Resort, resort, for merry play,
Call in Goliah, and he'll clear the way.

A room, a room, my gallant boys,
Give us room to rise.
Stir up the fire and give us light,
For in this house shall be a fight.
If you don't believe the word I say,
I'll call in Goliah, and he'll clear the way.

No. 2: Here comes I, Goliah, Goliah is my name,
With sword and pistol by my side, I hope to win the game.

No. 1: The game, sir, the game, sir, it's not within your power;
I'll slash you to inches in less than half an hour.

Nos 1 and 2 fight, 2 falls, and 1 breaks out in a lament.

No. 1: Alas! Alas! What's this I've done?
I've ruin'd myself, and kill'd my only son;
Round the kitchen, round the hall,
Is there not a doctor to be found at all?

One at the door says:

No. 3: Yes! Here am I, Johnny Brown,
The best doctor in the town.

No. 1: How came you to be the best doctor in the town?

No. 3: By my travels.

No. 1: Where did you travel?

No. 3: Hickerty, pickety, France and Spain,
Then back to old England again.

No. 1: What can you cure?
No. 3: Anything.

No. 1: Can you cure a dead man?

No. 3: Yes, indeed, that I can.

Holds a bottle to the slain champion, and says:

Rise up, Jack, and gight again.

The result being that he is resuscitated. No. 4 enters.

No. 4: Here comes I in old Row-rumple,
On my shoulder I carry a dumple,
In my hand a piece of fat.
Please can you pitch a copper into my old hat.

After this beggarly conclusion, and the singing of a song or two, the little actors, having obtained a donation, hasten off to the next dwelling. It would seem that these are boy-performers like the guisers in the Scottish Borders.

High Spen sword dancers, 1927.

Swalwell Sword Dance, 1910. (Photo: Cecil Sharp, from *Sword Dancers of Northern England*)

Sword Dancers

The long-sword dance with wooden links was an early tradition in Northumberland, Durham and Yorkshire and also found in the Shetlands and Scandinavia. The short-sword or rapper dance, using shorter links of flexible steel developed later, probably in the eighteenth century and was a highly skilled and competitive dance particularly associated with coal miners. The captain of the Earsdon team told Cecil Sharp just before the First World War that the short-sword tradition was at least a hundred years old.

James Wallace describes sword dancers in 1769 in the Hadrian's Wall area during the Christmas festivities. They were young men who 'march from village to village, and from house to house with music before them, dressed in an antic attire'. They are 'presented with a small gratuity in money, more or less, according to every house-holder's ability'. The leader, who does not participate in the dance, 'is distinguished from the rest by a more antic dress; a fox's skin generally serving him for a covering and ornament to his head, the tail hanging down his back'.

John Brand mentions frequently seeing what seems to be a long-sword dance in Northumberland and Durham in his *Popular Antiquities of Great Britain* (1795).

The *Bishoprick Garland* (1834) gives a lively and detailed description of what is probably a long-sword dance, with elements of a mummers' play:

> Sword-Dancers: It is still the practice, though less in repute than formerly, during the Christmas holidays, for companies of pitmen and other workmen from the neighbouring collieries to visit Sunderland, Durham, Newcastle, etc., to perform a sort of play or dance, accompanied by song and music ... The dancers are girded with swords and clad in white shirts or tunics, decorated with a profusion of ribands of various colours, gathered from the wardrobes of their mistresses and well-wishers. The captain generally wears a kind of faded uniform with a large cocked-hat and feather, for pre-eminent distinction; and the buffoon, or 'Bessy', who acts as treasurer and collects the cash in a tobacco-box, wears a hairy cap, with a fox's brush dependent ... The party assemble promiscuously, and the captain forms a circle with his sword, round which he walks and sings, each actor following as he is called on ...
>
> The dance then begins in slow and measured cadence; which soon increases in spirit, and at length bears the appearance of a serious affray. The Rector, alarmed, rushes forward to prevent bloodshed; and in his endeavours to separate the combatants, he receives a mortal blow and falls to the ground ...

> Captain: Oh for a doctor, a right good doctor!
> A ten-pound doctor, oh!
> Doctor: Here am I.
> Captain: Doctor, what's your fee?
> Doctor: Ten pounds is my fee; but nine pounds nineteen shillings and eleven pence three farthings I will take from thee.

> See here, see here, a doctor rare,
> Who travels much at home;
> Come take my pills – they cure all ills,
> Past, present, and to come!

> The plague, the palsy, and the gout,
> The devil within, and the devil without;
> Everything but a love-sick maid,
> And a consumption in the pocket.

> Take a little of my nif-naf,
> Put it on you tif-taf,
> Parson, rise up, and fight again,
> The doctor says you are not slain.

> The Rector gradually recovers, which is the signal for a general rejoicing. A general dance concludes the performance, to the old favourite tune of 'Kitty, Kitty, bo bo!'

There is an 1893 reference to sword dancers appearing before the duke at Alnwick Castle and in the streets of the town. Mrs Balfour was told of sword dances at Harbottle

Alnwick Castle. (Photo: Geoff Doel)

in the late nineteenth century by one of her servants and she also refers to the decline of the custom in her town of Belford:

> I have heard of the sword dancers going their rounds at Christmas in the neighbourhood of Harbottle, in the west of Northumberland where one of my servants lives; but the song is much abridged, the men are content to tie ribbons about their shirt sleeves and at their knees, the Bessy is dressed up very plainly as an old woman, and the 'dance' has lost most of its old steps. In Belford, the sword-dancers have not performed for about 10 years; but in December, 1890, five or six boys came round with masks, false noses or blackened faces and a broom. They repeated some incoherent and corrupted verses which neither rhymed nor made sense, and 'swept' the inhabitants of the house before them, till they were given money and cake. Since then none have come round. They appeared to call themselves the Besom Boys, or the Christmas Sweepers.

The Folk Archive Research North East (FARNE) website says that thirteen teams are recorded as appearing on a regular basis between 1850 and 1900 – Beadnell, Boghall, Blaydon, Chopwell, Earsdon, Hebburn, Houghton, Loughhoughton (Longhoughton), North Walbottle, Swalwell, Throckley, Widdrington, and Winlaton. Westerhope, Hetton-le-Hole, South Shields, High Spen and North Walbottle formed teams in the early twentieth century.

Cecil Sharp noted the short-sword dances at Swalwell, Earsdon, Winlaton and North Walbottle just before the First World War. Of the derivation of the short-sword tradition he comments:

Earsdon Sword Dance, the leader holds up the nut. (Photo: Cecil Sharp, from *Sword Dancers of Northern England*)

The invention of the intricate bi-circle type of dance figure must have been the product of extraordinary ingenious minds, and it is not easy, therefore, to explain its genesis by any theory of evolution. It would be easier to postulate the direct personal influence of some ingenious individual, and that at a comparatively late period in the history of the dance.

Sharp records that the dancers at Swalwell:

> … a populous mining village within a few miles of Newcastle, situated on the Durham bank of the Tyne perform annually on Christmas Eve and on the following days. There are five dancers, accompanied by the Captain, the Man-Woman Bessy, Betty or dirty Bet, who collects the money in a box, and a fiddler.

The Earsdon tradition was also on Christmas Eve and is also in traditional mining country. Again there are five dancers, the captain, the bessy and a fiddler. The captain remembered accounts of a tradition fifty years back of hanging the bessy, by encircling his throat with the lock of swords. This would make more sense if it was a long-sword tradition at that point as with short swords the aperture formed by the lock or nut when joined would be very small. The current calling-on song named the dancing heroes as the sons of Elliott, Lord Duncan, Nelson, Wellington and Buonaparte, but Sharp also collected an older version with type characters.

Sharp collected the Winlaton Dance in 1912, where the team was quite elderly – five dancers, a Betty and a musician playing a tin whistle. The calling-on song was similar to Earsdon. The Newcastle suburb of Walbottle had a sword dance custom from Bedlington imported in 1906:

> The sword dance, which is now annually performed at Christmas-time, was introduced there as recently as 1906 by a dancer of the name of Raine, who taught the Walbottle men the sword dance which usd to be, but is not now, danced at his native village, Bedlington … There are five dancers, a Tommy or Fool, a Bessy, and a concertina-player.

An engraving of Earsdon sword dancers, *c.* 1887. (From the *Monthly Chronicle* – 'North-Country Lore and Legend', 1887)

New Year Customs

New Year Customs indicate that First Footing was common all over Northumberland and Durham. The 'First Foot' had to be a 'dark man', and in some places unmarried, a 'fair man' being considered unlucky. It was obligatory for the First Foot to offer a gift of coal or a stick for the fire or a drink from 'his bottle'; in return he was given drink and cake. In the Borders the fire was never allowed to go out on New Year's Eve. In Durham there was the belief that nothing should be taken out of house on New Year's Day 'in case luck travels with it' so nothing was thrown away until the next day. To ensure prosperity in the coming year through sympathetic magic a householder checked that his larder was full and his coal and firewood stocks high.

Prohibitions according to the *Denham Tracts* are: never allow anyone to take a light out of your house on New Year's Day, as this will result in a death in the household during the year and never throw any ashes, dirty water, or anything, however worthless, out of your house on this day, for this is unlucky, but bringing in things is lucky. A female first visitant is disastrous. A children's song for money is recorded for New Year's Eve:

Get up, aad wife, & shake your feathers,
Dinna think that we are beggars;
We are but bairns come out to play,
Get up, and gie's wor Hogmanay.

Animal-Disguise Customs

These included dressing up in the hide of an ox.

The Allendale Tar Barrels on New Year's Eve

Traditionally the participants were all male and the custom began with guisers in home-made costumes meeting in the pubs; ladies are now involved. Shortly before midnight the guisers form a procession and carry blazing half tar barrels on their heads, marching behind the town band towards a great bonfire which is lit in the centre of market place and the fire barrels are thrown on it at midnight. The wooden barrels are about twelve inches deep and are filled with wood shavings soaked in paraffin. The guisers then First Foot to house parties.

Divination Customs

Divination was practiced on the solstices and at the New Year and, in Northumbria particularly, at the first New Moon of the year and particularly women divining their future husbands. The *Denham Tracts* refer to servant girls at Wooler tying their left-leg stocking round their neck in order to dream of their future husband. The ash tree, which has midwinter divination properties in several parts of the country, was also invoked in Northumbria. A leaf with equal divisions on each side was pulled off the tree and addressed as follows:

> Even, even, ash,
> I pull thee off the tree,
> The first young man that I do meet,
> My lover he shall be.

The leaf was then placed in the left shoe. And there is a proverbial saying: 'Even-ash, under the shoe, will get you a sweetheart'.

Apperley records that holly was also used for divination in Durham. Holly leaves were classified as male if they had prickles and female if they were smooth. For divination, she-holly leaves must be plucked on a Friday evening about midnight by persons who from setting out until the next dawn must keep silent. They should be collected in a three-cornered handkerchief and nine leaves should be selected and tied with nine knots inside the handkerchief and placed under the pillow to dream of one's future spouse.

St Agnes' Day (21 January) was a good day for husband divination. Two girls, each wishing to see their future husbands, must fast and be dumb through the whole of St Agnes' Eve. At night, in the same silence, they must make 'the dumb cake', aided by their friends, then divide it in two parts, one of which each girl takes, walks backwards upstairs, cuts the cake, and retires to bed. The dreams of the future husband should follow.

Girls also stuck a candle-end full of pins to bring their lovers to them, or, put an apple-pip in the fire whilst naming her lover. If it bursts with a noise he loves her, but if it burns silently he does not. If a girl wished to meet her future husband, she would carry an ash-leaf having an even tip, and say:

> The even ash-leaf in my hand,
> The first I meet shall be my man.

The game of 'keppy ball' at Alnwick is another divination custom, played by children. Mr Denham was told in 1861 at Alnwick that there used to be a coban or coven tree near the castle and he was told the surviving rhyme and its explanation:

Keppy ball, keppy ball, covine tree,
Come down the lang loanin' and tell to me,
The form and the features, the speech and degree,
Of the man that is my true lover to be.

Keppy ball, keppy ball, coban tree,
Come down the lang loanin' and tell to me,
How many years old (her name) is to be –

One a maiden, two a wife,
Three a maiden, four a wife,
Five a maiden, six a wife, &c.

And so on, the odds for the single, the even numbers for the married state so long as the ball can be kept rebounding against the tree round which they play. There were similar tree customs elsewhere in the North and Borders and the title 'covine tree' seems to mean 'trysting tree' and therefore to be a tree marking meetings.

Valentine's Day

There is evidence of Valentine cards being sent in Northumbria in the late eighteenth century and some of the verses have been collected, for example:

The ring is round, the bed is square,
You and I shall be a pair.

Some draw valentines by lot,
And some draw those that they love not;
But I draw you whom I love best,
And choose you from among the rest.

The second rhyme refers to the practice of Valentine parties when lots were drawn for partners for dancing and feasting.

St George's Day Custom, Morpeth

One of the young men in the town to be St George, and all the rest of the young men to attend him; and upon St George Day, all come to church, and at the rehearsing of the creed to stand up and draw his sword.

Collop Monday

This was the day before Shrove Tuesday and was the last day meat could be eaten before Lent and usually consisted of 'collop' a slice of dried, salted and hung meat preserved through the winter. Rashers of bacon were carried to houses of friends. There was also a strange custom of carrying from house to house an effigy of Jesus in a coffin and asking for money in exchange for seeing it.

Shrovetide Customs

In Catholic times people were shriven in the morning of Shrove Tuesday, which immediately preceded Lent, a penitential period of fasting. Having taken the day off, men engaged in violent customs such as cock-fighting and street football in the afternoon before the more peaceful pastimes of Lent. These traditions continued after the Reformation until suppressed by the Victorians. Because eggs were forbidden in Lent, a 'pancake bell' was once rung in Morpeth parish church and Durham and Newcastle Cathedrals, to warn housewives to use up their stocks of eggs – hence the origin of Pancake Day.

Some Roman Catholic households opened their kitchens and neighbours and passers-by were permitted to enter and fry a pancake from food supplies left to hand. In Durham children still believed that pancakes fell from the mouth of the Cathedral knocker.

Shrovetide Football has been recorded as played at Ford, Rothbury, Wooler, Chester-le-Street, Alnwick and Sedgefield.

At Ford single men played married men in a football match known as 'The Gaudy Loup'. An account of 1889 says:

> It was customary in the last century for men of Ford village, every Shrove Tuesday evening, to play a football match, married *versus* single. The village at that time stood very much nearer the church than it does now – in fact under the very shadow of Ford Castle – and we are told, the married men played towards the church, and the unmarried from it. Before commencing the match, all the men who had been married during the previous year were compelled to jump over, or wade through, the Gaudy Loup; otherwise they were not allowed to join in the game. The custom long ago fell into abeyance, and now it is entirely forgotten.
>
> The Gaudy Loup was a pit filled with water, and generally full of rushes, that stood somewhere on the site of the plantation known as Neville's Plantin', and in close proximity to the Delaval's cock-pit. The Castle Quarry in this plantation – so called from supplying the stone for the rebuilding of Ford Castle by – eventually swallowed up this pit, and another, and the last 'gaudy loup' was found in a field on Ford Hill Farm, which field is now glebe land, on the south of Ford Rectory.
>
> The Sedgefield Shrove Tuesday Football match has been played on the green at least since the twelfth century. It can last for hours and gets rowdy; the object is to 'allay' the ball and get it in the part of the village defended by the other side. It is said to have started from a quarrel between Chester-le-Street apprentices and a retainer at Lumly Castle, the first football being the latter's Head.

Brand describes the Alnwick football match of 1762:

> The castle waits came playing to the castle at 2 p.m. when a football was thrown over the wall to the populace congregated before the gates. Then came forth the tall, stately porter dressed in the Percy livery, blue and yellow, plentifully decorated with silver lace, and gave the ball its first kick, sending it bounding out of the barbican of the castle into Bailiffgate; and then the young and vigorous kicked it through the principal streets of the town, and afterwards into the pasture, which had been from time immemorial for such enjoyments. Here it was kicked about until the great struggle came for the honour of making capture of the ball itself. The more vigorous combatants kicked it away from the multitude, and at last some one, stronger and fleeter than the rest, seized upon it and fled away pursued by others. To escape with the ball, the Aln was waded though or swam across, and walls were scaled and hedges broken down. The victor was the hero of the day and proud of his trophy.

At Wooler, the game was played between the married and unmarried men; and after kicking the ball through the town, one party endeavoured to kick it into the hopper of Earl Mill, and the other over a tree which stood at the 'cook of the Till'. In days of yore, this contest sometimes continued for three days.

At Morpeth it was an Easter tradition – on Easter Monday and Tuesday the young people resorted to the North Field to play ball, 'doun the lang lonnin' and other games. Hist BNC, xiv, 129.

The *Newcastle Daily Chronicle* 6 March 1889 recorded:

> Mr Joseph Murray, of Newcastle, as the representative of the Murray family, who have provided the ball for sixty-five years, duly appeared at one o'clock, with the ball in his hand. Immediately he threw out the ball the fun became fast and furious, and contrary to all the traditions of the game, the ball went rapidly up street, all the efforts of the Down-Streeters failing to stay the attack of the Up-Streeters, who seemed bent upon making a strong bid for victory. Right away the ball went upwards, only to be checked again at the King's Head: then it did not stop until reaching Red Rose Hall. There, a change took place; the Down-Streeters made a big effort, and, by the aid of vigorous play on the part of a few fresh hands, conspicuous among whom was a well known 'county-back', the ball was brought rapidly down street, and its progress was no checked until it was shot into the half-frozen river Cone. Plunging in, through the ice and gushing waters, several adventurous players succeeded in getting the ball once more into play, at the expense of a thorough wetting. In a few minutes' time the ball was again forced into the river, and this time several youngsters got it upon the ice and tried to play it there, only to drop through the ice at very soft places, and to lose the ball through the holes into the water, all of which caused immense amusement to the spectators. The ball went up street after a terrific struggle, and there it remained, in spite of the herculean efforts put forth by the Down-Streeters. A few minutes before six o'clock the ball was returned to Mr Murray, who addressed the multitude from the window of the Crown Inn, congratulating them upon the magnificent struggle there had been. An announcement was subsequently made that next year a cup would be given to be held by some responsible person on behalf of the winners.

Netherwitton Easter Tuesday Holly Bussing

Notes & Queries for May 1857 records:

> The lads and lasses of the village and vicinity met and accompanied by our worthy parish
> clerk, who plays an excellent fiddle ... proceed to the woods to get holly, with which some
> decorate a stone cross that stands in the village, while others are 'bobbing around' to 'Speed
> the Plough' or 'Birnie Bouzle'.

Carling Sunday is the fifth Sunday in Lent and at Alnwick, Newcastle-upon-Tyne and
Belford people went to the pubs to spend their carling-groat, the landlords providing
the carlings, 'which are steeped grey pease, fried, well-buttered, peppered, salted'.
Mrs Balfour of Belsay reported:

> At Harbottle, near Rothbury, I am told by one of my servants, who comes from that
> district, the Carlings are served in a great bowl in the middle of the table, and little is eaten
> besides; but it is a point of honour to finish all the peas, and the person who gets the last
> one will be the first married. I have had them prepared correctly for my own table; they are
> first steeped for twenty-four hours, then boiled for two or three hours; then fried in butter;
> lastly, just after being put into a bowl, they were well sprinkled with sugar, and a glass or
> two of rum was poured over them.

Easter Customs

Good Friday food included hot cross buns, which are spiced tea cakes marked with
a white cross. Sunderland wives once gave them to their sailor husbands as a charm
against shipwreck. In Durham there was a belief that bread baked on this day would last
for a year. 'Fig-Sue' was a traditional dinner dish and comprised figs, ale, white bread,
sugar and nutmeg.

On Easter Sunday parishioners tried to wear something new to church, children
in particular wearing new clothes. Those not wearing new clothes were in danger of
being targeted by the birds. People rose early hoping to see the sun rise and dance.
At Stamfordham it was believed that the sun when rising dances on the water. William
Hutchinson mentions the giving of dyed and gilded eggs to children called 'Paste Eggs',
a corruption of Pasche Eggs, and there are references to this at Morpeth and Alnwick.
Mrs Balfour recounts the pace-egging tradition at Belford in the mid-nineteenth century:

This is still a common custom. The Belford children come regularly 'a-pacing', and
ask, 'Please to gi' a paste egg'. It is not everyone, however, who gives them eggs; but they
are content to get sweets, halfpence, etc, and some people – especially at the farms – lay
in a stock of gaudily-dyed boiled eggs for them.

On Easter Monday dyed hard-boiled 'paste eggs' were rolled, symbolic of
resurrection. A favoured way of dying them was by wrapping and boiling them in onion
peelings; each locality had its favourite rolling place and there were often competitions.
In Durham girls were allowed to pull off the caps of the boys.

May Day

John Brand remembered being awoken by a woman selling May Garlands and singing on the streets in Newcastle-upon-Tyne:

> Rise up, maidens! Fy for shame!
> For I've been four long miles from hame;
> I have been gathering my garlands gay,
> Rise up, fair maids, and take in your May.

Doors and mantelpieces were decked with greenery and young people would go into the fields before breakfast to wash their faces in May dew, which was thought to be good for the complexion. William Hutchinson describes this and the collection of hawthorn and the use of a primitive maypole:

> The young people of both sexes go out early in the morning of the 1st day of May to gather the flowering thorn and the dew of the grass, which they bring home with music and acclamations; and having dressed a poll on the town green with garlands, dance around it. The dew was considered as a grand cosmetic and preserved the face from wrinkles, blotches, and the traces of old age.

> …The syllabub, prepared from the May feast, is made of warm milk from the cow, sweet cake, and wine; and a kind of divination is practised by fishing with a ladle for a wedding ring, which is dropped into it for the purpose of prognosticating who shall be first married.

> The custom of dressing out stools with a cushion of flowers on May Day formerly prevailed in this district. A layer of clay was placed on the stool, and therein was stuck with great regularity an arrangement of all sorts of flowers so close as to form a beautiful cushion. They were exhibited at the doors of houses in the villages and at the end of cross lanes, where the attendants begged money from passengers to enable them to have an evening feast.

Royal Oak Day

This was the local name for Oak Apple Day, 29 May, which was a public holiday from the Restoration until the early nineteenth century, with a church service in the morning, followed by a free afternoon. In Newcastle-upon-Tyne the Royalist and Roundhead factions were perpetuated in folk custom. The Royalists wore oak leaves in their hats on this day and placed them on their horse's heads, proclaiming 'Royal Oak, the Whigs to provoke!' Their opponents retorted 'Plane-tree leaves; the church-folk are thieves!'

At the grammar school, the boys were up before 3 a.m., and with their band of wind instruments, went round the town to collect all the boys, and thence to the chapel wood, where they cut large branches of oak. They then marched to the school, which they ornamented with the oak. The master heard the lessons and gave holiday after 8 a.m. This was an old custom and a continuance of that of the companies.

Mystery Plays

In the Middle Ages Northumberland and Durham celebrated their religious and civic festivals with great processions and colourful rituals, in which the streets were decorated, singers and musicians entertained the crowds and dazzlingly colourful processions wound their way through the narrow medieval streets. Perhaps the greatest medieval festival was that of *Corpus Christi* (Thursday after Trinity Sunday) when from each church a procession of clergy, choir, parish members and guildsmen promenaded through the streets. It was for this festival that the civic guilds began to erect pageants in the streets and have their guild members play out select scenes from the Old and the New Testament. The pageants (funded entirely by the guilds though the playlets were possibly written by clergy) were a form of advertisement and propaganda, for each guild took over a biblical scene which had some pertinence to their trade, the bakers taking the Last Supper, the nailers the Crucifixion, the shipwrights Noah's Ark etc. Depending on the number and wealth of the guilds in a town, dozens of pageants and hundreds of actors, could have been involved and the plays are thought to have been performed several times through the day.

During the reign of Elizabeth I the performance texts of these 'Mystery' or *Corpus Christi* plays were ordered to be sent to London to be examined by the Queen's religious and political advisors. They were never returned and were presumably destroyed. All that remains from the northern Mysteries are the vestiges of one Newcastle play, *Noah's Ark*, referred to by early scholars as 'the Shipwright's Ancient Play' and in which the principal characters are God, an angel, Noah, Mrs Noah and the Devil. God opens the play with a long monologue in which he explains his resolve to destroy mankind – with one exception – 'all but Noah, my darling free'. An angel messenger is accordingly sent to Noah bidding him:

> Go, make a ship
> Of stiff board and great,
> Although he be not a wright.

Noah with perfect obedience and humility accepts God's will:

> I am six hundred winter old;
> Unlusty I am to do such a deed
> For I have neither ryff nor ruff,
> Spyer, sprond, spront, nor sproll–
> Christ be the shaper of this ship,
> For a ship needs make I must.

Midsummer Fires on St John's Eve

It was customary to make a large bonfire on Midsummer Eve, surrounded by dancers and merrymakers and, as the flames died down, couples who wished to be lucky jumped over the embers.

Sir Benjamin Stone gives an excellent Edwardian account of the St John's Eve Bonfire celebrations at Whalton, with photographs (some of which are reproduced in this book):

I. BRINGING IN THE FAGGOTS
Until comparatively recent times a bonfire was lit on St John's Eve in several Northumbrian villages, and is still at Whalton, which, remote from rail and tramway, retains most of its old customs. There the fire has never been omitted within the memory of the oldest inhabitant. It has been postponed owing to heavy rain, but never left out of the year's round of observances.

As Midsummer approaches much wood is marked out for the bonfire, sometimes with the consent of local farmers. When this has been cut, it is brought into the village with a certain amount of formality. On the evening of the 4th of July a cart is borrowed and loaded with branches and faggots, some of the men get into the shafts, more are hooked on by means of long ropes, and then, with a good deal of shouting and horn blowing, the lumbersome vehicle is run down into the village.

II. BUILDING UP THE FAGGOTS
Two loads of faggots, as a rule, are brought into the village, always by hand; no horse is ever used. Then begins the building of the bonfire, which, for some unexplained reason, is always constructed on the same spot. The site does not vary a yard from year to year; and yet nobody knows why this particular place is chosen.

III. READY FOR LIGHTING
While the building is in progress a remarkable scene takes place. Of a sudden every house empties, all the villagers turning out with one accord. Old men and women, middle-aged couples, youths and maidens, school lads and lassies, toddlers in short frocks-the whole populace appears; and presently groups are gathered everywhere to watch the stacking of the bonfire.

Later on the children, joining hands, form a moving ring round the pile, and dance till they are tired. They are keenly interested in the ceremony, because they always have a scramble for sweets, which are scattered for their special enjoyment.

IV. VILLAGERS DANCING
Youths and maidens also dance in the neighbourhood of the pile, a fiddler or other instrumentalist providing the music.

V. THE FIRE ALIGHT
As darkness creeps over the countryside, and the shades of night blot out familiar details, there is a cry of 'Light her!' The bonfire, like a ship, is invariably personified, and of the feminine gender. A moment later a flame leaps skywards, to be joined by another, and then another, till at last the whole village is illuminated. The Baal fire burns!

Beyond dancing, there is no subsequent festivity or ceremony. But, if local tradition may be trusted, there used to be some superstitious practices. People jumped over the fire and

Bringing home the faggots for the Baal Fire. (Photo: Sir Benjamin Stone)

Hellfire Tender at Whalton, Northumberland, 1903. (Photo: Sir Benjamin Stone)

through it. In bygone times, too, stealthy appropriation of ashes was not uncommon. Both these circumstances point in the same direction–to the remarkably long continuance of ancient rites and uses of fire.

In the 1880s, Revd Elliott Bates, wrote in a paper for the Berwickshire Naturalists' Club that:

On Midsummer's eve, reckoned according to the old style, it was formerly the custom of the inhabitants, young and old, not only of Whalton but of most of the adjacent villages, to collect a large cartload of whins and other combustible materials, which was dragged by them with great rejoicing (a fiddler being seated on the top of the cart) into the village and erected into a pile. The people from the surrounding country assembled towards evening, when it was set on fie; and while the young danced around it, the elders looked on smoking their pipes and drinking their beer, until it was consumed.

The Northumberland Baal Fire – Building up the faggots, 1903. (Photo: Sir Benjamin Stone)

The Northumbrian Baal Fire ready for lighting, 1903. (Photo: Sir Benjamin Stone)

The rector also mentioned people jumping through the fire.

> There used to be a similar custom at Bamburgh. And in Elsdon where cattle were driven though the bonfires. In Sunderland in the mid-nineteenth century, fires were built in the streets on Midsummer night and people lept over the flames. At Morpeth youngsters of both sexes beat each other with branchs of rowan tree.

Durham Miners' Gala

On the third Sunday of July the streets still fill with marchers and bands and banners and there is a service in the cathedral.

Harvest Customs – The Northumberland Kern Baby

Sir Benjamin Stone writes:

> Till recent years a rather common form of the revelry and thanksgiving which have ever
> taken place at the ingathering of the harvest was the Kern, though it has now died out
> everywhere except in a few Northumbrian villages.
>
>   One of the customs of the festival of Ceres, it had many local variations. It was observed
> in the northern part of Northumberland at the close of the reaping, not the ingathering.
> Immediately the sickle was laid down and the last sheaf set on end the men shouted that
> they had 'got the kern.' Then a curious image was produced – an image dressed in a white
> frock with coloured ribbons and crowned with corn ears-stuck on a pole, and held aloft by
> the strongest man of the party while the rest circled round it. Subsequently it was taken to
> the barn, set on high, and the merry-makers fell to on the harvest supper.

A Corn Dolly
from Whalton,
Northumberland. (Photo:
Sir Benjamin Stone)

Though the Kern baby, as the figure was generally called, is seldom seen nowadays even in Northumberland, it is still made at Whalton. The village effigy, which is about 2ft in height, is taken to church, and is afterwards the presiding genius at the harvest festivities.

Sir Benjamin Stone's photograph of the Kern Baby at Whalton is reproduced in this book.

The Durham 'Mell Doll' was akin to the Northumbrian Kern Baby (from the Norse *mele* meaning corn) and the Harvest Home was known as 'The Mell Day' in Durham, referring specifically to the final day of reaping. According to the *Denham Tracts*, the reapers were accompanied by a fiddle on the last day and there was dancing amongst the sheaves. Apperley says, 'the last sheaf used to be dressed in finery and crowned with wheatears, hoisted on a pole, and all the harvesters danced round this … harvest queen, who afterwards presided over the supper.

When the last sheaf had been tied the head man cried out:

Blest be the day that Christ was born,
We've getten 't mell of Mr —'s corn;
Weel bound, and better shorn.
Hip! Hip! Hip! Huzza!! Huzza!!

Then the labourers were given beer (often laced with rum). Mr Denham writes that, 'In the years 1825 and 1826 I saw the reapers come home from the Mell Field in the evening, dressed in high crowned muslin caps, profusely ornamented with ribbons of various colours, and preceded by music'.

Mr Denham mentions the discontinuance of the Harvest Supper and says that the dancing at the end of the suppers in the old days were attended by 'Mummers' – 'men and women disguised in each other's apparel'. Farmers replaced the suppers by a bonus called the 'Mell Shilling'.

Writing about the Mell:

Houghton Feast began in the time of Queen Mary. Bernard Gilpin, the rector/priest at Houghton – arranged for bullock to be killed and with that & other things feasted the poor. Because of his sympathies with Protestantism an order arrived that Gilpin was to be executed in London. Gilpin was travelling to London for that purpose when his horse fell and Gilpin broke his leg. He lodged with an innkeeper and while he was recuperating news arrived that Queen Mary had died and had been succeeded by the Protestant Queen Elizabeth. The new monarch speedily sent out orders that all clergymen then under arrest were to be freed. After Gilpin's death the feast continued to be celebrated – it falls between 5–10 October.

The *Monthly Chronicle* (1889) lists other summer feasts and activities enjoyed by communities:

Wakes, church ales, summerings, tides, rush-bearings, revels, gants (ie village fairs or wakes) hoppings, fairs, vigils, ale feasts or Whitsum ales, are anniversary feasts, great numbers of which are still kept in the counties of Durham and Northumberland in all their primitive glory and rude yet hearty hospitality, in commemoration of the dedication of the parish church or parochial chapel to some patron saint. Hopping is derived from the Anglo-Saxon 'hoppan' to dance or leap. Dances in the country villages of the north of England are termed hops at the present period of time. By an act of Convocation passed in the reign of Henry VIII, the Feast of the Dedication was ordered to be held on the first Sunday in October, and the celebration of the Saint's Day to be laid aside …

In the county of Durham a series of local feasts begin in the last Sunday in July, and proceed, I think, in the following order: Neasham, Hurworth, Aldbrough, Stapleton, Blackwell, Cockerton, Haughton-le-Skerne, Harrowgate, Burdon, Sadberge, Coatham, Brafferton and Aycliffe. Duck-hunting, racing, drinking, banqueting, and all sorts of secular sports are the order of the day on the Sabbath and a day or two after or during. The city was not without its hoppings. 'Gallowgate was one of the districts of Newcastle that had the privilege of holding a 'hopping' – or rural fair, with its shows, merry-go-rounds, and other diversions of a homely character, mixed with a great deal of dancing, or 'hopping' whence the name. It was held every year at Whitsuntide.

Riding the Stang

Riding the Stang was a street entertainment irregularly performed (it is to be hoped) in which communities in the North took steps to publicly reprimand and shame individuals who had 'misbehaved' sexually or had otherwise committed some kind of offence. The 'Stang' was a piece of stout pole or paling. There follows an eye-witness account:

I witnessed the custom of riding the stang at Staindrop in the county of Durham, in the year 1831 … A too confiding damsel, having loved 'not wisely but too well', found herself involved in the troubles of maternity, before she had secured a husband, and had, therefore, to obtain from the magistrates an order for maintenance which she saddled on a young fellow of the 'ne'er-do-well' class.

Young Graceless did not, however, ever relish having the honours of paternity thrust upon him; nay, he resented the 'soft impeachment' and even went so far as to say that an official of the church (the verger) was the real Simon Pure; and, in consequence, he and his friends made it very hot and uncomfortable for the poor fellow. Amongst other things provided for his annoyance was riding the stang, which I witnessed.

First, towards evening a large quantity of straw, sticks, faggots and all sorts of combustibles were piled up in the market place, near the Butchers' Shambles. Then, after dark, a group of men paraded about the streets and lanes ringing a bell, probably borrowed from the town crier for the occasion, and as they proceeded the numbers increased till they had all the rabble of the place collected round them. They then went to a shed outside the town, and there procured a cart, whereon thy placed a ladder crossways. On the ladder they set up an effigy of the verger in his church gown, and this was supported by young Graceless, who carried the bell and acted as fugle-man, on one side, and by a friend on the other. Willing hands were ready to draw the cart as they entered the town, with the bell ringing, the crowd thumping on pans and kettles, whistles and trumpets, sometimes groaning, sometimes hurrahing; just as it took their humour. As soon as they were fairly within the

Riding the Stang. (From the *Monthly Chronicle – 'North-Country Lore and Legend'*, 1887)

street, there was a halt; the bell was rung for silence when young Graceless in a loud voice, harangued them in a doggerel, some lines of which are too coarse to be repeated.

Then off they went, brawling, groaning and making all the uproar possible, for a hundred yards or so. Then another halt and repetition of the oration. And thus they went up one side of the street and down the other, taking care to stop in front of the most prominent houses, particularly those of the clergymen and others connected with the church, and giving the verger's house special attention.

About ten o'clock they drew up in the market place, and the effigy was made fast to a stake in the pile of faggots. Young Graceless again orated; and then the fire was applied, the bell rung, the pans rattled, and the crowd yelled and danced round the flaming mass.

No one interfered with them; indeed, there was neither mischief nor danger. It was altogether a vulgar, low exhibition, and certainly more honoured in the breach than the observance.

Riding the Stang was not always an exercise in punishment. From Denham we learn:

In the pit villages near Gateshead Fell there is another variety of 'Ridin' the Stang' not meant as a mark of disgrace, as it is in many others; on the contrary, it is rather a mark of honour. The morning after a young man is married he is mounted upon a board or pole, and carried to the public house upon the shoulders of two man, where he is expected to give the pit's crew a 'blaw out'. The last married man is always chosen mayor, and undergoes the same operation. Both these events produce gaudy days.

They myed me ride the stang as suin
As aw show'd fyace at wark agyen.
The upshot was a gaudy-day,
A grand blaw-out wi' Grundy's yell.
(Wilson's *'Pitman's Pay'*)

Gaudy Days

Another irregular custom had the delightful name of Gaudy Days or alternatively Cuckoo Mornin'; there is a parallel here with the two days which followed New Year's Eve in Scotland and which miners often took as an unofficial holiday and which they regarded as a right. The *Denham Tracts* comment:

> In the pit villages near Gateshead Fell, there are certain times of the year when the young men and lads refuse to work, and insist on a 'gaudy day'; for instance, the first morning they hear the cuckoo, and when the turnips and peas are in maturity. They call these periods 'a cuckoo mornin', 'a tormit [turnip] mornin', and 'a pea mornin'. At such times they frequently adjourn to a neighbouring public house, where they enjoy themselves during a great part of the day.

Hallowe'en

The History of Alnwick (1813) reports:

> On this evening it is customary for the young people to dive for apples. A tub is filled with water and each of the party throws in an apple. When the apples are all in the tub, the party, each in his turn, attempts to take an apple with his mouth out of the water, it not being allowed to catch the apple at the side or suck it into the mouth. The party must, therefore, dive, and take it from the bottom. Catch at the apple (generally called 'Catch the Candle') is another diversion on this evening. A piece stick is suspended by the middle with an apple stuck at one end and a lighted candle fixed at the other extremity. The stick is twirled about, and the parties, with their hands behind their backs, catch at the apple with their mouths by turns.

In Durham an old custom was to eat an apple before a mirror, and the lover's face will be reflected therein; but on no account must the worker of this spell look backwards. This of course originated as a divination custom, as did the custom of throwing nuts into the fire. If the nuts burn together it is a hopeful sign for love and marriage, but if they jump apart it is not propitious for union of the sexes.

ELEVEN
LORE &
SUPERSTITIONS

Superstition is defined as a belief or reverence of things or rituals which, because it is often based on assumptions and ignorance, should be accepted as irrational and illogical. But old ways die hard in the North East and we know a great many people (ourselves included) that pick up pins and 'touch wood' for luck, hang up horseshoes and avoid walking under ladders, yet these rituals are as naught compared to the quantity of Durham and Northumbrian beliefs and superstitious rituals of yesteryear.

We are fortunate in that numerous Victorian and Edwardian men and women made efforts to record the traditional beliefs and lore (i.e. stories) of the North East which were fast disappearing and published their findings in various journals and magazines. This kind of evidence is easily accessible and a vital source of interest and information, even though the material has been modified and sanitised for a middle-class, somewhat prudish, literary audience. For example, pre-Victorian collectors often noted that many customs and rituals involved intemperance, debauchery, money collecting and the occasional riot, but this kind of comment is generally lacking in the compilations of vicars and educated middle-class women in the Victorian and Edwardian period. Other kinds of bias can be detected in the works of such collectors as Henry Bourne, a Newcastle vicar, who published his *Antiquitates Vulgares or the Antiquities of the Common People* in 1725. His violent anti-Catholicism is immediately apparent and behind his research is a desire as a religious leader of the community to eradicate or at the very least modify those customs and superstitions in the countryside which appear to him to have an overlay of 'the Old Religion'. At the same time he appears genuinely to appreciate that many of the old rituals afford innocent pleasure to the men women and children in a parish.

Every age in recorded literature has its beliefs, superstitions and rituals. Sometimes this is only apparent in archaeology. In the disturbed time of the rievers in Northumberland apotropaic signs were crudely incised into the stonework around the windows of pele towers by those who were trying to defend their homes. Particularly favoured were triangles (representative of the power of the Trinity), and the equal-armed or St Andrew cross as symbols of the protective force of Christ and his saints. They were intended magically to

Above: Elsdon pele tower. (Photo. Geoff Doel)

Left: Preston Tower which has apotropaic marks over the windows. (Photo: Geoff Doel)

avert danger of attack and death, particularly by burning, for the marauders often stacked up fires by the ground-floor wooden door in order to gain access to the room in which beasts had been herded, and fires were then often spread deliberately to the floors above.

In the early Christian era, Bede, writing in the eighth century and without appearing censorious, tells us how the cross erected by Oswald at the Battle of Heavenfield in the seventh century was afterwards chipped away by pilgrims to the site, who used the chippings in water as medicine for men and beasts. And when the cross had totally disappeared, the earth on which the cross had stood was taken away to be used as medicine. Bede tells us that there was a hole 6ft deep where the original cross had once stood. In Bede's day, Church authorities were debating whether charms, spells and the naïve folk-magic rituals of the people were potentially evil and whether they should be prohibited or simply tolerated. The country people certainly invoked the names of deities older than Christianity, such as Woden and Thor, as part of their spell and charm making.

At a much later period, the seventeenth century, it is of interest to note how many old spells and charms from Northumberland and Durham, especially those designed to ward off disease or to effect a cure, often petition the Trinity or the saints and contain scraps of pre-Reformation liturgical prayer, while it is known that holy water taken from the church or bits of candles that had burned before the altar were often 'acquired' surreptitiously from the parish church to be used in spell making.

Our records mostly cover the period from the end of the eighteenth century to the years of the First World War. Durham and Northumberland very often shared the same superstitious ideas, but there were many variations even within the one county, and country traditions were often different (usually more energetic) and endured longer than those of the towns. We have divided the following collected aphorisms into the usual sections: The New Born, Marriage Customs, Death Rituals, etc.

The New Born

Pregnancy was never discussed openly in a family and once the midwife had been sent for, other children in the house were sent to relatives or neighbours to get them out of the way. Though there was no way then that a mother could determine the date or moment of her child's birth everyone knew that a May baby would never be a healthy child, if it was born an hour after midnight it would be psychic, and if born with a caul it would always be lucky. To have such information was to be forearmed.

No one pulled a dress or vest over a tiny baby's head until it was christened, so it was dressed by having the garment drawn up over the feet. Though the baby was carefully washed, the inside of its tiny hands were not in case it 'washed the luck away'. Sticklers for the old rituals maintained its right hand should not be washed for a year. The nails were not cut for a year; if they were the child would become a thief. Mothers trimmed them by biting them. Once the child reached the toddler stage, the nails were never cut on Friday or Saturday; these are unlucky days. Before taking a child out of the birthing room the midwife or a female relative ensured by sympathetic magic that the baby would never go 'downhill'. If there was no staircase leading upstairs the woman took the child in her arms and stood on a chair or stool 'thereby assuring it a rise in life'.

Even a poor family tried to get a cake and a cheese before the birth of the baby. The moment all were assured that mother and baby were going to survive, the cheese and cake were cut, and everybody ate some. It was said that this prevented the child growing up ugly. One portion of cake and cheese was kept back and en route to the christening was given to a passing child of the opposite sex to that of the newborn.

Often a number of babies were brought to the church for christening at the same time. When this happened it was accepted that the baby boys must be christened first – otherwise the girls would grow beards. Baptism was thought to be good for a child for 'children never thrive till they are christened'. No one wanted a baby to remain silent during its christening for that meant it would die soon. A bawling baby during a christening was an excellent sign and it was said that 'the devil is going out of them'.

Every mother knew better than to call a newborn baby by its name until the child had received it at the church. Many children died either during the birth process or soon afterwards and, no matter how tempting, it was important to avoid naming the new baby after a dead brother or sister. This was extremely unlucky and could bring about the child's death – or bring bad luck upon its head so that it would never prosper.

After childbed, the mother's first outing must be to church, otherwise it was said she would bring ill-luck to the first house she entered.

At a baby's first showing in another house it should receive no less than three presents. These were known as its 'almison'; they are traditionally an egg, some bread, some salt, and occasionally a piece of money. Apperley tells us 'The bread and salt are things used in sacrifices; the egg has always been a sacred emblem; the money is for luck, and should be carefully kept'. Mothers are advised never to rock a cradle even accidentally when it is empty or it will rock another baby into it. If the newest baby cuts its teeth early another baby will soon be on the way; Hence the proverb, 'Soon teeth, soon toes' (i.e. another set of them). If a tooth appears first in baby's upper jaw, that means death in infancy (not necessarily the baby's own). When a baby tooth is lost, the cavity was filled with salt, and the tooth thrown into the fire while reciting the charm:

Fire, fire, burn bane,
God send me my tooth again!

A family cradle must never, ever be sold. It can, however, be passed on.

Baby's hair should always be cut when the moon is waxing, and all its clippings and combings burnt. If the hair burns briskly when thrown into the fire, it means a long life; a smouldering hair is a sign of death. Anyone swallowing a hair will die soon for it wraps itself round the heart.

If a mother has several children she must ensure that no older child jumps over the new baby's head otherwise the infant will be of stunted growth. If a seventh son is born, he will be a doctor; if a woman has seven daughters all in a row, the seventh child will be a witch.

Boys & Girls

Durham schoolboys used to make a cross of straw or twigs when they saw a rainbow. This was said to 'cross out the rainbow'.

In Confirmation, any child who is touched by the bishop's left hand will never get married.

Marriage Customs

Once the decision was made to marry, it was important that the couple choose a lucky day and season for 'the big day'. Lent and May were to be avoided as these were considered unlucky for weddings. On no account was the bride to hear the banns given out, or her children would be born deaf and dumb. The bridegroom usually had to endure an old custom – being 'ragged' on the eve of his wedding. These ragging customs varied but one example is that the bridegroom's friends ran after him, caught him, pinned him down and physically stripped off his boots and socks and washed his feet in a specially prepared basin of hot water. During the ordeal he was required to reward them with a few silver coins dropped into the basin for beer-money.

What we think of as a traditional white wedding dress did not become popular until the Victorian period – and only then an exclusive fashion for the wealthy. Most women simply wore their best clothes – but certain colours like black and green were always shunned (green was the colour of the fairies, black indicated mourning and was inappropriate). Women guests likewise did not wear anything green. Everyone knew the old adage:

Something old, something new,
Something borrowed, and something blue.

Everyone hoped that the sun would come out on the day of the marriage, for 'happy is the bride whom the sun shines on'.

There were several rituals involving dressing the bride; no Durham girl for example looked at herself in the mirror once she was dressed for church – it was tempting fate and no one wanted to be jilted at the altar. As she left her parent's house a white favour or an old shoe was thrown after her for luck. There were town and country ways of celebrating a wedding. In the more rural areas the bridal party usually walked to church, escorted by the male members of the two families and male neighbours armed with guns, which they continually fired. The bridegroom meanwhile had to leave his parent's house and undergo the ritual of being bombarded by shoes thrown by well-wishers. Denham tells us that this was still regularly done in the early nineteenth century. 'When a young person is leaving his family and friends or going to be married, it is still usual to throw an old shoe after him for luck. Many try to hit the party on the back'.

Mackenzie informs us that the religious ceremony itself was not without its more hilarious moments, especially in country areas, 'There was once an ancient and indecent custom when during the marriage service young men attempted to unloose and pluck off the bride's garters which were then borne in triumph round the church'. Before the couple left the church the bride was kissed by the clergyman who had conducted the service – it was his privilege.

Once the bridal party had exited from the porch a thin currant cake was presented to the bridegroom, which was marked in squares. Now the bridegroom took up a position behind the bride and broke the cake after which a portion of the cake and a plate was thrown 'for luck' over the bride's head. '[The cake] thus hallowed it is thrown up and scrambled for by attendants to excite prophetic dreams of love and marriage'.

The cake throwing was followed by sustaining 'hot-pots' or 'possets' for the whole party to taste, usually provided by the bride's family. During this refreshment the bride removed her left stocking and threw it over the party – whoever caught it would marry next. One Victorian folklorist, obviously disapproving of these vulgar country customs tersely observed, 'Stocking throwing is now obsolete'. In some areas it 'was formerly the custom to address complimentary verse to the bridal couple before they left the church. This was called "saying the Nominy". The verses differed, were of no great poetical merit, and always ended with "pray remember the Nomine sayer".'

Victorian folklorists tells us that 'At St Helen's Auckland, and other villages, the "race for the bride-door" for a ribbon or kerchief is still customary while in Durham, when a wedding party arrives from church, pennies are thrown from the upper window of the bride's home and scrambled for'.

In some parts of Northumbria after the marriage ceremony it was customary for some brides to jump over a petting stool (usually a wooden bench or 'louping stool') put in her path as she left the church – in some places it was a petting *stone* which was obviously *in situ* in the churchyard or nearby. A portable petting stool was often placed in the gateway. Helped by groom and attendants she had to jump over and clear it. If successful, she ensured good luck in her marriage; failure to clear it was an indication of an ill-temper. Holy Island had an actual stone and guns were shot as the bridal party

Holy Island showing St Cuthbert's Bay and the sixteenth-century fort built by Henry VIII on a volcanic plug. (From Sir Walter Scott's *Marmion*, 1855 edition)

moved towards the petting stone. Brides still sometimes go through this ceremony on Lindisfarne.

Belford (a late nineteenth-century account) says that:

> ... the Petting Stone is now represented by a stool in charge of a widow and taken to the church door when the wedding takes place. The keeper of the stool (the widow) gets a small sum of money. Men who jump the bride over the stool have the right to claim a kiss.

An interesting account comes from Belford Workhouse in the Victorian period:

> Where marriages before the Registrar take place, the inmates improvise a petting-stool by putting a bench across the door, over which they will not help the bride till some money has been given them. As in all cases, there is something to be mounted on, climbed or jumped over.

From an article by Cuthbert Home Traslaw in 1889 we learn:

> Within the recollection of old people, still living the bridegroom was required, on occasion of a wedding at Ford Church, to jump over, or wade through, the 'Gaudy Loup', or forfeit money to be expended in drinking the health of the newly-married couple. The 'Gaudy

Loup' being some distance from the church the paten stick seems to have been eventually found more convenient. The stick was placed before the church door when a newly married couple was leaving the sacred edifice, and the bride, as well as the bridegroom was required to leap it or forfeit the usual money.

There are few details of rituals enacted once the bridal party had returned home. One custom appears to be very old, that of the couple's friends being given broken white bread soaked in hot milk into which the wedding ring was dropped; 'the bride and bridegroom tasted the contents then the bowl was taken up by lasses and lads; whoever fished up the ring first would be married next'.

Until mid-Victorian times a bride was often conducted to her bed by her bridesmaids and flung her (remaining) stocking with her right hand over her left shoulder – 'whichever caught it would be the next bride'.

Some allied superstitions

In the days before electric lighting, candles were regularly used as a magical device for looking into the future. A bright spark in a candle was an indication that a love letter was about to arrive. Snuffing out a candle by accident means a marriage is imminent. Piercing a candle through the wick while it is burning conjures up the image of a lover.

> It's not the candle alone I stick,
> But ....'s heart, I mean to prick;
> Whether he's (she's) asleep or wake,
> I'll have him (her) come to me and speak.

It was also said that if you stumble by accident going upstairs you will be married within the year. A cat sneezing before a wedding means good luck for the couple. Those who always guess the time correctly will never be married.

If a loaf breaks in the hand while it is being cut, a man and his wife will soon be parted. And the loss of the wedding-ring meant the loss of a husband's love.

Death Rituals

People in the North East believed in a range of portents which presaged death. In Durham dogs howling, jackdaws or swallows coming down the chimney, the image of a 'winding sheet' in the candle, the crowing of a cock at dead of night, birds hovering round the house, resting on a window-sill or fluttering against a window pane, three raps 'given by an invisible hand', were all indications that someone in the household would die shortly. Northumbrian 'death omens' included; a cock crowing on a threshold, magpies on the doorstep, the fall of a photograph, double-yoked eggs, three crows, a diamond shape in a folded table cloth and boots accidentally put on a kitchen table.

Dreams often signalled that a death was imminent or had taken place: if you dreamt of the loss of a tooth you would soon hear of the death of a friend; if you dreamt of a wedding it meant that someone near you had died. Sit thirteen persons down to a meal together, and one of them will die before the year is out.

Should you shiver inadvertently it means that someone is walking over your grave. If you broke a looking-glass it occasioned bad luck for seven years – or meant the death of someone in the house. Along the coast it is said that if you turned a loaf of bread upside down while cutting it a ship would be wrecked with loss of life; three candlesticks on the table had the same causal effect. Do not point at the stars and certainly do not attempt to count them for this will occasion your own death.

In the eighteenth, nineteenth and early twentieth centuries relatives nearly always died at home in their own beds. In the North East certain ritual actions, sympathetic magic, were enacted to help the departing spirit 'on its way'. Because it was believed that no one could die on a bed or pillow stuffed with pigeon or game feathers it was important to make sure that the pillows and mattress were not of the sort that could delay death needlessly. At the moment of death the door was opened to show the departing spirit the way out. Along the East Coast it was claimed that people usually 'gave up the ghost' during the falling of the tide.

Female relatives washed and 'laid out' the corpse, but always had the help of neighbours. The best linen was used. The death-room was then shrouded in white sheets, the clock was stopped and the looking-glass was covered 'to show that for the dead time is no more and earthly vanity departed.' It also prevented any reflection of the ghost. In some communities a plate of salt was placed upon the breast 'as an emblem of eternity'.

Neighbours and relatives were invited in to see the corpse and touch it or kiss it, a 'token that they are in peace with the dead'. Not to do this would bring on dreams of the dead. The corpse was regarded with some anxiety, for as Denham tells us, 'if the flesh and joints of a corpse retain their softness and pliability, it portends, it is said, another death, if not in the household at least in the same family, in quick time'.

When it came to burial, many Northumbrian women chose (as in Scotland) not to attend the graveside. Applerly explains the rituals concerning the route to the grave – as a mark of respect men would always remove or tip their hat as the funeral cortège passed:

> The coffin must be carried to the church by the old-established 'church-road,' and the notion still prevails that the way over which a body is carried to its burial thereby become a highroad. Therefore, in the case of private roads or bridges (the Prebend's Bridge at Durham, certainly) a small toll is levied when a funeral procession passes over it. The [male adult] coffin bearers are usually chosen so as to correspond with the deceased in sex, age, and position. In the case of children and young girls, white scarves and gloves are worn; and if the dead person were a young unmarried woman, a 'maiden garland', used to be laid on the coffin, and hung up in the church after the funeral … when arriving at the churchyard, the dead must be carried to the grave by way of the sun (east, by south, west, and north), for 'ye wad no hae them carry the dead again the sun; the dead maun aye go wi the sun'…

No one minded rain because there was an old saying, 'happy is the corpse that the rain rains on'.

Finally, the bees were told of their master's death, and asked to accept a new one, or they would all die, and the survivors tried to contain excessive grief as this would hinder the corpse.

Common Superstitions

Garments: In the past certain actions were seen as luck bringers. Superstitions regarding dress were manifold. If you accidentally put on a garment inside out, that brought good luck; the mistake must never be rectified or the luck will be turned. However, if you put a button or hook into the wrong hole while dressing in the morning, something unpleasant will happen to you during the day. A little child (boy or girl) putting on a dress for the first time which has a pocket should have some money put into it by his father; this ensures the child's future prosperity. Say to a woman who is wearing a new dress, 'I wish you health to wear it, strength to tear it, and money to buy another'. When a young apprentice or tradesman first puts on his apron, say 'Weel may ye brook your apron'. This, if said by a lucky person, will ensure his success in life. A spider on your clothes means that money is coming to you. If the hem of your dress (this is for ladies or cross-dressers) persistently turns upwards, a letter is coming your way. If your apron should fall off, someone has you in mind. If you are wearing clothes that need mending at work you will lose money.

Animals

In Durham if a black cat enters a house, it must by no means be turned away, for it is a luck bringer especially for those seeking love: 'Wherever the cat of the house is black/ The lasses of lovers will have no lack.' In Northumberland they believe that black cats, white heather and piebald horses are luck bringers.

In Durham it is lucky to see an early lamb, though only if its head is turned towards you, but in Northumberland it is lucky to see a sheep facing the wind. If the hens come into the house, a visitor is on his way. Whenever you hear the cuckoo, turn the money in your pocket; it means you will have money all that year. Sadly, if your pocket is empty, it will remain so the whole year.

Although the raven is considered an unlucky bird in Northumberland, in Durham they remember the story of Sir John Duck and how a raven, by dropping a gold piece at his feet when he was a poor out-of-work butcher boy, turned his fortune. Duck ended up as an extremely rich owner of coal mines, and in his memory coals are often called 'ducks' in Durham.

A spider falling on you from the ceiling means a legacy is coming your way. Goats kept about an inn or farmstead is not only conducive to the health of other domestic animals, but brings good luck to the owner. 'The magpie is usually considered an unlucky bird because it would not go into the ark with Noah; it sat outside 'jabbing at the drowned world'. When you see magpies repeat the rhyme 'One is sorrow, two mirth/ Three a wedding, four a birth/ Five heaven, six hell /Seven the de'il's ain sel'. However, if you see a single magpie you can say 'Magpie, magpie, flutter and flee/ Turn up your tail and good luck come to me'. And all will be well.

Kittens born in May are unlucky and useless. Hedgehogs suck cows' udders and drink up all their milk as they lie asleep. Do no touch a toad as it is poisonous. 'When setting hens, the number of eggs should be odd; if the number be even, you will have no chickens'. A rook that deserts a rookery is forecasting the downfall of the family on whose property it stands. If swallows leave a place where they once nested it means ill luck for those that live there. A hen that crows like a cock brings ill luck, 'just as does a woman who whistles'. If you meet a white horse make a wish and don't look back. It is unlucky to hear a peacock screech and peacock's feathers should never be brought indoors. If a toad crosses your path it will rain. On the first day of every month say 'white rabbit' before anything else and the rest of the month will be lucky. Horseshoes are lucky but don't carry a horseshoe upside down or the luck will spill out.

Personal

If you have eyebrows that meet you are fortunate; a mole on the neck is also a luck bringer, for it means health to the owner. Always enter a house right foot first; to enter with the left foot brings ill luck to those within; to repair the mistake go back and enter again. If your eyes are weak, have your ears pierced. 'Spitting for luck' is still commonly done. The 'luck of three' is an old belief – if you fail twice in trying to do a thing, you will succeed the third time. They have an old saying, 'The third time's catchy time'. Finding a pin is always lucky:

> See a pin & pick it up,
> All the day you'll have good luck;
> See a pin & let it lie,
> You'll need a pin before you die.

It is unlucky to lend or give a pin to anyone. They may take one of yours, but should not thank you.

If your nose itches, someone or something will annoy you. If your foot itches you will travel. If your left hand itches you will have to pay out money; an itchy right palm means money is coming to you. If your left ear tingles, someone is defaming you; a tingling right ear means that someone is speaking well of you.

Do not wash your hands in a basin at the same time as someone else; you are sure to quarrel before the day is out. To dream of water means you will hear of sickness. It is unlucky to start on a journey then be called back. The saying 'sing before breakfast, cry before supper', means that unusually high spirits signify some coming misfortune.

Taboos

Spilling salt is ominous, but you can amend your luck by throwing a pinch of salt three times over your left shoulder with your right hand. Never cross a knife and fork on a plate. Never give a knife to anyone as a present, it is said to 'cut love'. Never begin anything on Friday, it will not prosper.

Never walk under a ladder, or if you must, cross your fingers and wish or spit. If you have walked under a ladder and are with someone, wait for him to speak first, and any ill luck that may be coming will fall on his head. Hawthorn blossom ('May') must never be brought into the house. Never turn a mattress on Friday or Saturday. Never open an umbrella in the house. Never hang a picture over the door. Never kill a spider. Never look at the new moon through a glass or trees. Never accept salt from someone's plate. If they offer say 'Help me to saut, help me to sorrow', and this will avert danger. Never give a pair of gloves to your sweetheart (Durham only) for 'you'll never get the hand you glove'. If you see a glove on the ground leave it alone and you'll escape bad luck. If you drop your glove let someone pick it up but do not thank them.

We have to add that many of the above are patently untrue or anti-social – hedgehogs for example do not suck cows' udders; toads are not poisonous; spitting is an unpleasant and unsophisticated practice.

Forecasting the Weather

Weather forecasts are very reliable today, but in the past countrymen in the North had to learn to read the weather signs such as, 'A bruff (ring) round the moon means bad weather and so does a curlew' or, 'If the leaves remain long on the trees in autumn, it is going to be a hard winter'. An old favourite is 'watch the cat as she washes her face, and if she passes her paw over her ear it will rain tomorrow'. 'If it rains on Friday, it is sure to rain on Sunday', hence 'wet Friday, wet Sunday'. 'When rooks feed in the street a storm is at hand'.

If the wind blows on New Year's Eve:

If on New Year's Eve the night wind blow south,
It betokeneth warmth and growth;
If west, much milk, and fish in the sea;
If north, much cold and storms there will be;
If west, the trees will bear much fruit;
If north-east, flee it, man and brute.

If Candlemas Day be fair and bright,
Winter will have another flight;
If Candlemas Day be clouds and rain,
Winter is gone, and will not come again.

Some prophesied the coming weather from that of the last three days of March. These are called 'the borrowing days'.

March borrowed from April
Three days and they war ill;
The first o' them war wind and weet,
The next o' them war snaw and sleet,
The last o' them war wind and rain,
Which gar'd the silly puir ewes come hirpling hame.

The oak and ash trees were also considered to prophesy the weather:

> If the oak bud before the ash
> We shall be sure to have a splash;
> But if the ash bud before the oak,
> We shall have weather as hard as a rock.

Spells, Charms & Curative Rituals from Durham

Until the National Health Service was established poor country people and even the farmers as well as many of the urban poor simply could not afford doctors. There was little for them to do except consult a local wise woman or man with a reputation for healing and knowledge of herbal medicine. Midwives were also consulted. How effective they were will never be known. Apperley in *Folk-Lore of the County of Durham* claims that there was a remedy for most diseases in the shape of a spell or a charm. It is to be noted that 50 per cent of the charms she collected have to do with curing beasts.

> Whooping-cough may be cured by passing the child under an ass … In Sunderland, the crown of the head is shaved and the hair hung upon a bush, so that birds, carrying it to their nests, may take the cough with it. For epilepsy, a half-crown may be offered at Communion and then asked for again, and made into a ring to be worn by the person affected. For cramp, garter the left leg, below the knee, or tie an eel's skin round it. A most unpleasant remedy is that for a wen for the touching of a corpse's hand will cure it.

Andrew Mill's Stobb (gibbet) was once thought sovereign against toothache. Warts can be charmed away by taking a piece of raw meat (it ought to be stolen) rubbing the warts with it, and throwing it away. As the meat decays the warts will vanish. If anyone is bitten by a dog, the animal should be destroyed, for, should it go mad at any time, the person bitten would be attacked by hydrophobia. If it is found difficult to rear calves, the leg of one of the dead animals, should be hung in the chimney.

'To work as though one was working for need-fire', is a common proverb in the North, and refers to the practice of producing fire by the friction of two pieces of wood. This was done when the murrain prevailed among cattle and the diseased animals were made to pass through the smoke raised by this holy fire. This was considered a certain cure. When cattle have foul in the feet, the turf on which the beast treads with the affected foot is taken up and hung in the open air. As it crumbles away, so will the diseased foot recover. The water in which Irish and other stones have been steeped has been used in the bishopric as a cure for disease for cattle.

Denham, Egglestone and others have written about the use of stones, sticks and teeth particularly in Durham when used as curatives in the eighteenth, nineteenth and early twentieth centuries:

> Stones with perforations in them … are variously called 'holed stones', 'charmed stones', 'holy stones', 'hag stones' and 'snake stones'. They are suspended to the tester of a bedhead to prevent the nightmare. They are also placed over the backs of cows or other beasts as an

efficacious remedy and preventive of the malady called 'hoose' or 'huse'; that is difficulty of breathing. These stones may be considered holy or sacred in a twofold sense; first, because they have a hole through them; and secondly, because like holy water, they are equally beneficial in keeping all sorts, kinds and descriptions of evil spirits at a safe distance. Note: These stones to be at all efficacious must be holed naturally. One hung over the head of a horse will prevent its sweating in the stable.

Not many years ago it was a popular belief that a stone brought from Ireland possessed the virtue of curing cattle that had the misfortune to have been envenomed by the bite of an adder … Not only were Irish stones held in high estimation as charms, but Irish sticks were likewise prized. The farmer who dwelt in a valley infested with adders was fortunate if he possessed an Irish horse or an Irish cow; a tooth of the former would as effectually neutralise a sting as an Irish stone or stick, and a touch from the cow was equally efficacious. If a native of Ireland made a circle with his finger around a reptile, it died.

In the month of October, 1884, I handled a once famous Irish stone which was in the custody of a good dame residing beneath the shadow of the Old Abbey of Blanchland in Northumberland. On enquiry being made for the charm, a search was made in the corner of a drawer, and a bag, yellow with age, was carefully brought out, unfolded, and in its contents – the Irish stone – exhibited. The good lady was eighty eight years of age, and the charm was in the house when she married into it, forty nine years before. It was the property of her husband, who died about twenty-nine years since, and she had heard him say that the stone belonged to his father. During her time it had been 'lent all up and down' to individuals who had got envenomed or had cattle suffering and she could testify that its application stopped inflammation, as she remembered effectually rubbing the face of her husband who had been stung by a bee. The charm, which, as she had heard came from Connaught is a water worn flint, lentiform, of a dark colour, blotched with white.

Irish sticks: These were also held in high estimation for their healing powers. Seventy years ago, Wearsdale possessed one owned by a person named Morley:

An elderly woman, now dead, gave me the following particulars respecting herself and the wonderful stick.

When a scholar in the village school she had a ring worm on her arm, and the mistress of the school rubbed the part affected with her gold wedding ring, a supposed remedy; but the wedding ring charm failed, and the scholar was despatched to Morley's. The famed stick, which had a great reputation in the valley, was brought into operation and as far as my informant could remember a cure was affected.

Sixty years ago an innkeeper's daughter, at St John's Chapel, got stung in the hand whilst working in the garden. The hand was cured by the application of an Irish stick, which was about five inches long and an inch thick. It was well polished, through repeated operations, and the charm remained at the public house for many years, having almost as much practice as the village doctor.

The teeth of an Irish horse: These were evidently as efficacious as stones and sticks:

Seventy years ago [c. 1819] peats were largely used as a fuel by the dwellers in the higher reaches of the Wear Valley. A Weardale resident informed me that he remembered a lead miner's wife, who, whilst stacking peats, or in local parlance *mooing* peats in the yard, had her hand envenomed by some reptile which had been amongst the peats when brought in from the moors. A neighbour, hearing of the good woman's misfortune, sent an Irish horse tooth with the instructions to rub it over the envenomed hand. The order was obeyed, a cure affected, and the tooth, having added to its reputation as a charm, was kept as such for many long years afterwards.

The Lee Penny:

The Lee Penny is actually a stone described as dark red in colour, triangular in shape and its size about half an inch each side. It is supposed to have been in the possession of the family of Lockhart of Lee since 1329 [and obtained in] the Holy Land. Napier … writing in 1879 stated in his book on folk lore that it is … 'still in possession of the Lee family'. The plague broke out Newcastle 1645 [and it is recorded] … that the inhabitants sent for the Lee Penny. It did so much good that they offered to pay the money and keep the charm … It cures all diseases in men and cattle, and the bite of a mad dog both in man and beast. It is used by dipping the stone in water, which is given to the diseased cattle to drink and the person who has been bit and the wound or part affected is washed with the water. Many cures claimed to be performed by it; people came from Scotland and as far as Yorkshire to get the water in which the stone had been dipped.

Pit superstitions

Coal once made Britain wealthy, but miners working in the Northumberland-Durham coalfields in the eighteenth and early nineteenth centuries had jobs that were dirty and dangerous. Coal had to be laboriously hacked out of the seams with picks and shovels and dragged in trolleys along narrow galleries to the bottom of the pit-shaft where it could be raised to the pithead. The men worked long shifts and were poorly paid. They disappeared down the mines like trolls and when they reappeared they were covered in coal dust and walked home in the dark hungry and exhausted. Women and children also worked long shifts underground, the women pulling the trolleys in the dark, until laws were passed in the mid-nineteenth century forbidding this kind of employment. No safety regulations were enforced at this early period and pit disasters were common with shafts caving in or flooding and gas causing explosions underground. Most of the pitmen's superstitions are to do with signs, inauspicious omens and portents which are telling him not to go to work that day.

It was considered unlucky for a pitman to meet a pig or a woman on his way to work. If he was on night shift and he meets a woman *en route* for the pit he must return home. Whatever shift he is on he must turn back if at any time is he meets a woman with a white apron (pitmen's wives used to don a white apron if they were laying out a corpse or attending the sick).

If there is a crow sitting on the pulley wheel he should not go down the shaft. He must also return home if he sees a white rabbit or a hare. It is unlucky to have to return home for anything, so the pitman should not go back straight away but should sit down for a short time. If the bowl of his pipe breaks off there will be an accident.

Fishermen

Fishermen in the North East were notoriously superstitious and quick to call off a fishing trip if something inauspicious occurred.

If a fisherman meets a woman going down to his boat it is unlucky. If she steps over his nets or lines that means even greater misfortune. Boulmer fishermen considered it unlucky to meet anyone carrying water. Before the Boulmer fishing cottages were given running water, the village girls collected water from wells, but because of the men's superstition the women did not fetch water until all the boats were off the beach.

Holy Island fishermen turn back if they meet a pig, a priest dressed in black, or an old woman. The same fishermen believe it unlucky to bring ashore a dead body which they have found floating.

For all fishermen the word 'pig' must never be said as it is unlucky. If it has to be mentioned at all it is called something else such as 'the thing'. Meeting a pig (some say a black pig) before a trip will have it called off. In cutting a loaf if it is turned upside down a ship will shortly be in a similar position.

TWELVE
SONGS OF THE PEOPLE

Northumbria claims the biggest range of traditional songs and music of any English region, including: border ballads, lyrical songs, occupational songs, plus a vast range of dance tunes traditionally composed for fiddle and small pipes, but later adapted to button instruments such as accordions and concertinas. There are medieval carvings of a harper and a bagpiper in Hexham Abbey. A living tradition has been partly sustained by a strong tradition of publishing ballad and folksongs going back 250 years. Newcastle-upon-Tyne was an important centre for the printing of broadside ballads as well as song collections, though many of these ballads were not of local origin.

John Peacock, named in the song 'Winlaton Hopping' (i.e. fair), played the Northumbrian small pipes in the 1830s and was called 'the Paganini of the North'. He was among the last of the Town Waits maintained by the burgesses of Newcastle-upon-Tyne, employed to play at the Mayor's Gala occasions and who also supplemented their income by playing at weddings and village dances.

There was an extensive revival of the Northumbrian pipes in the late twentieth century lead by the shepherd Joe Hutton, Colin Ross and Kathryn Tickell, the latter taking the pipes to a much wider popular audience.

There is a magnificent tradition of border ballads in the region and, as with the dance tunes they are inextricably linked with Scottish songs and music, just as the border clans ranged on both sides of the border, seeing themselves distinct from both England and Scotland. The ballad of *Chevy Chase* (possibly about the Battle of Otterburn (1388) was first mentioned in 1540 and Sir Philip Sidney famously wrote in his *Apologie for Poetrie* (published posthumously in 1595):

> I never heard the olde song of Percy and Duglas, that I found not my heart mooved more then with a trumpet: and yet is it sung but by some blinde crouder, with no rougher voice, then rude stile; which being so evill apparelled in the dust and cobwebbes of that uncivill age, what would it worke, trimmed in the gorgeous eloquence of Pindar!

The first ballad collection featuring the region is that of Bishop Thomas Percy (who claimed to be descended from the Northumberland Percies), who in 1765 dedicated

A carving of a bagpiper, Hexham Abbey.   A carving of a harpist, Hexham Abbey.
(Photo: Geoff Doel)   (Photo: Geoff Doel)

his *Reliques of Ancient Poetry* to 'Elizabeth, Baroness Percy and Duchess and Countess of Northumberland' and he deliberately included many ballads with Northumbrian and Border connections such as: 'The Ancient Ballad of Chevy-chase'; 'The Battle of Otterbourne'; 'The Child of Elle'; 'Adam Bell, Clym of the Clough, and William of Cloudesley'; The more modern 'Ballad of Chevy-chace'; 'The Rising in the North'; 'Northumberland Betrayed by Douglas' and 'Child Waters'. Both Sir Walter Scott's *Minstrelsy of the Scottish Border* and Francis Child's *The English & Scottish Popular Ballads* feature ballads from the region, including some taken from Percy and from Scottish collections.

The first song collections of the region, *Gammer Gurton's Garland* and *The Bishoprick Garland* (specifically on Durham) were compiled and printed by Joseph Ritson, and he seems to have collected some of the songs himself, including 'Elsie Marley' and 'The Keel Row'. John Bell's *Rhymes of Northern Bards* (1812) featured 'The Hexhamshire Lass'; 'Buy Broom Buzzems'; 'The Water of Tyne' and 'Bobby Shaftoe', the latter referring to the relationship of Robert Shafto Esq., of Whitworth and Miss Bellasyse the heiress of Brancepeth. Michael Denham reports a portrait of Shafto, complete with yellow hair, in the mansion of Whitworth Park, and he cites an early version of the song:

Bobby Shaftoe's bright and fair,
Combing down his yellow hair;
He's my ain for ivvermair,
Hey for Bobby Shaftoe.

Bobby Shaftoe's gone to sea,
Wi' silver buckles at his knee;
When he comes back he'll marry me,
Bonny Bobby Shaftoe.

Denham further reports an extra verse added at electioneering time if there was a Shafto candidate:

Bobby Shafto's looking out,
All his ribbons flew about,
All the lasses gave a shout –
'Hey' for Bobby Shaftoe!

Bell collected, but did not print, many of the tunes. William Shields of Swalwell, musical director of the Covent Garden Theatre, published some Border tunes about 1817. James Telfer collected songs in the region in the 1840s, including 'The Death of Parcy Reed' and 'Willie o' Winsbury'. William Oliver noted many of the tunes in 1855. The region is particularly strong in work-related songs and children's songs such as 'Dance Ti Thy Daddy':

Dance to your Daddy, my little laddy
Dance to your Daddy, my little man.
Thou shalt have a fish and thou shalt have a fin
Thou shalt have a codlin when the boat comes in.
Thou shalt have a haddock baked in a pan
Dance to your Daddy, my little man.

Northumbrian Minstrelsy (1882) was the first large regional collection of songs and was assembled over many years, even before the Society of Antiquaries appointed a committee of White, Fenwick and Kell to do the collecting and assembling. The famous antiquarian John Collingwood Bruce and John Stokoe edited the final edition. The ballads featured in it come mainly from printed sources (some outside of Northumbria) and are well anotated. Less information is given about the songs individually, though Ritson, Bell and Telfer are prominent sources; little information is given on the singers. Well-loved Northumbrian songs such as 'Blow the Wind Southerly' (first published in 1834); 'Bonny at Morn'; and 'I Drew My Ship into a Harbour' are included.

The most important modern collection is A.L. Lloyd's 'Come All Ye Bold Miners' (1952), which although a national collection, strongly features the North East, and had an outstanding introduction and notes. It contains an impressive and grim collection of explosion and disaster ballads reflecting the danger of the occupation and many songs about work and labour disputes, including the remarkable 'The Black Leg Miners', collected as recently as 1949 from the singing of Mr W. Sampsey of Bishop Auckland:

Oh, early in the evening, just after dark,
The blackleg miners creep out and go to work,
With their moleskin trousers and dirty old shirt
Go the dirty blackleg miners.

They take their picks and down they go,
To dig out the coal that's lying down below,
And there isn't a woman in this town row
Will look at a blackleg miner.

Oh, Delaval is a terrible place,
They rub wet clay in the blackleg's face,
And round the pit-heaps they run a foot-race
With the dirty blackleg miners.

Oh, don't go near the Seghill mine
For across the mainway they hang a line
To catch the throat and break the spine
Of the dirty blackleg miners.

They'll take your tools and your duds as well
And throw them down in the pit of hell.
It's down you go and fare you well,
You dirty blackleg miners.

So join the union while you may,
Don't you wait till your dying day
For that may not be far away,
You dirty blackleg miners.

In 2001 the University of Newcastle launched a 'folk and traditional music performance' degree, the first of it's kind in England and Wales. This has been spectacularly sucessful and will help to ensure the survival of the rich heritage of traditional music and song in the North-East.

THIRTEEN

GAZETTEER OF LEGENDS IN THE LANDSCAPE

The following is a list of other traditions not included in the book so far.

Alnwick – The Dirty Bottles of the Market Cross Inn

A man died whilst cleaning these bottles, which can be seen in the front window of the pub and they are said not to have been touched since.

The Grey Man of Bellister Castle

There is a tradition mentioned in Richardson's *Table Talk* of the castle being haunted by a spectre which presages calamity to the Bellisters. A suggested cause is the killing of a visiting harper who had the dogs set on him, after which his ghost pursued the lord of the castle when out after sunset.

Berwick

On 14 Oct 1881 a terrible and sudden storm devastated the east coast, drowning hundreds of fishermen, including many from Eyemouth. Neighbouring Berwick suffered little if any loss of life. According to James Petrie, grandson of the Harbour Master of Berwick, this was beccause his grandfather had refused to let the fishermen go to sea because the barometer indicated bad weather. The fishermen protested, but their lives were saved.

The Lang Man of Bollihope

Two giants formerly used to live in the high Weardale moors. They stood as tall as towers with arms like tree trunks and had great shaggy beards. When thy stamped their feet the very steeples shook. When they sat down the noise was like thunder in the hills. One evening the locals felt the ground shake. They ran out of their houses to see what the commotion was and saw the giants striding towards each other purposefully over

Above: The Market Cross Inn, Alnwick.
(Photo: Geoff Doel)

Right: The 'dirty bottles' window, Alnwick.
(Photo: Geoff Doel)

Berwick. (Photo: Geoff Doel)

Bollihope Common. A quarrel started and then the fight began. Each giant wielded a great club. The battle was over when one giant was felled and the victor strode off. The villagers ran to the site thinking to see the dead giant's body but all that remained was a mound of stones, now known as 'The Lang Man of Bollihope'.

Blanchland Abbey

There is a tradition that a party of Scots on their way to despoil the medieval monastery of white canons were surprised by a mist and unable to discover the trackway to Blanchland. They wandered vainly for some time over the fells, and had come to the Dead Friar's Hill on the Durham side of the Derwent, when they heard the sound of bells which the cannons were ringing for joy at their supposed deliverance. Thus guided to the abbey, they broke through the gates, set fire to the buildings, and after slaughtering several of the brethren, rode off with much spoil. Historically the chronicler Froissart mentions the burning of the abbey by the Scots under Earls of Murray and Douglas and their pursuit by Edward III:

> ... he ordered his army to be prepared, and turned his horses to feed in the fields near to a monastery of white monks, which had been burnt, and which was called in King Arthur's time, Blanche Land. Then the king confessed himself, and each made his preparation according to his abilities. The king ordered plenty of masses to be said, to housel such as were devoutly inclined. The following day the English army, with trumpets sounding and banners flying attacked the Scots.

Brinkburn Priory
An Augustinian priory south-east of Rothbury in a loop of the River Coquet, has a similar legend to that of Blanchland, recounted by Stephen Oliver (W.A. Chatto):

> Tradition reports that a Scottish army, which had made a predatory incursion into England, passed near Brinkburn on their return homeward without observing the priory; but that hearing the bells, which the monks had begun too prematurely to ring for joy at their escape, they turned back and plundered the place.

There is said to be a unique fairy cemetery near the priory church.

Broomley Lough
Richardson's *Table Book* mentions a prince, earl or chieftain who sank his treasure in the Lough and to secure it he engaged a wizard who put the strong box under powerful spell. There is a saying that when the wind in stormy weather agitates the waters of the Lough 'they were ever still and unruffled above the place where the treasure lay'.

The Charlton Spur, Hesleyside
The Charlton Spur is on the south bank of the Tyne opposite Charlton. The lady of the great house was reputed to serve up the spur on a platter when the larder was empty, a story painted in Wallington Hall by William Bell Scot. The Charlton Spur is six inches long with a rowel two inches in diameter and in possession of the Charlton family.

Chillingham Wild Cattle
A herd of white cattle (descendents of prehistoric wild oxen) roam though the well-wooded dells of Chillingham Park. According to the *Monthly Chronicle*:

> They are said to be the stock that ran wild amid the forest and hills of ancient Northumbria, and their shaggy appearance even now is both picturesque and formidable. The Prince of Wales paid a visit to Chillingham in October, 1872 when it was announced that he would signal the occasion by shooting the noblest specimen of the herd. His Royal Highness allowed himself to be stowed away in a hay cart that was carrying the poor creatures their breakfast, and was thus able, from the hungry and unsuspecting herd that followed him down, to exterminate the king bull at leisure. The plan, no doubt, was in accordance with

Chillingham Castle. (Photo: Geoff Doel)

courtly notions of safety ... but it was scarcely a feat to warrant any unusual jubilation. A few hours after the tragedy, the carcase was brought from the scene of slaughter, and carefully deposited on the castle lawn.

The Consett Giants

There were three giants whose names were Cor, Ben and Con. Their home was the hills round Consett and they were smiths. The hill tops functioned as their smithies and their anvils were the great boulders that littered the hills. They had only one hammer but they passed this between them; they flung this through the air sometimes as far as nine miles as it passed from one giant to another. But the giants had been placed under a spell, for should the hammer ever drop to the ground they would all vanish. One day Con was sitting on his wind-swept hilltop near Consett when his brother Ben threw him the hammer. It was only a distance of two miles but Con's eyesight had so deteriorated that he could not see it coming. He held out his hand guided only by the noise. Although his fingers briefly touched the handle, it slipped out of his grasp and jettisoned to the earth. At that point all three giants disappeared from the earth. At Howden near Consett, there is a very deep valley created by the hammer when it fell to the ground and skimmed along the earth.

Cuddy's Cave

Cuddy's Cave, Belford was an occasional resting place of St Cuthbert and may be one of the resting places of St Cuthbert's coffin.

Cuddy's Cove (or Cave)

On the south side of Dod Law in the Cheviots, is cave named after Cuthbert, who is supposed to have sheltered here when he worked as a shepherd. Above this is a stone block where the Devil is supposed to have hanged his grandmother.

Cuddy's Crags

Cuddy's Crags are east of Houseteads, Hadrian's Wall

The Devil's Causeway

The Devil's Causeway is the nickname given to Ermyn Street (i.e. an old Roman road), which ran from Halton Chesters east of Kirk Heaton, over the Wansbeck, east of Hartburn Church, in a straight course between Nether Witton and Witton Shields, to Brinkburn Priory. It crossed the Coquet a little below the priory, at a place where the remains of the piers of the Roman bridge were perfectly distinct, 'particularly the ashlar work on the north side, covered with elm trees', as a learned correspondent wrote to Mackenzie in 1824. The Causeway proceeded over Rimside Moor, crossing the Aln below Whittingham, passed Shawdon and Glanton (where it was locally known as the Deor or Deer Street) to the Till, near Fowbey, then by Horton Castle, Lowick and Ancroft to the Tweed, which it crossed at Corn Mills near West Ord, a little above Berwick.

Dunstanburgh

The little, coloured quartz crystals found in the cracks of the crag are known as 'Dunstanburgh Diamonds'. The noise of the Rumble Churn, near the castle, is said to be made by demons.

Erneshow or Eagle's Hill

The *Monthly Chronicle* says:

> Here also was the oratory of St Michael held sacred in former days for its power over inveterate diseases & likewise protected by the virtue of the saint from being plundered who if they dared meddle with it were punished with madness so that they roved wildly about mangling their limbs until they died.

The Fairies' Kettle

The Fairies' Kettle, near Marsden in one of the limestone caves, is a circular hole in the rock about 5ft deep. The sea covers this at spring tide and often leaves a pool of water in which fish are left swimming.

The Farmers' Folly, Alnwick

The 83ft high column (the Percy Tenantry Column) surmounted by a Percy lion with his stiff outstretched tail is locally known as 'The Farmers' Folly'. Locals still tell the story that the duke was enraged to find his tenants were rich enough to offer such a tribute and raised their rents accordingly. This is definitely just a legend, though a good example of pithy and ironic Northumbrian humour.

The Farnes

Murray's *Northumberland, Handbook to Durham and Northumberland Part II* says:

> When St Cuthbert first came to Farne he succeeded in banishing the evil spirits which had hitherto held undisturbed possession of the principal island; but they retreated no further than the Wedums, as the wide opens were then called, whence their shrieks were

plainly audible. St Bartholomew and his attendant monks used to see them 'clad in cowls and riding upon goats, black in complexion, short in stature; their countencances most hideous; their heads long; and the whole band most horrible in appearance'. In later times a belief that these islands are haunted has arisen from the fact of shipwrecked sailors being buried here.

Walcott's *The East Coast of England* (1861) also mentions this tradition:

> Beyond Farne are the Noxes, and E. and W. The Wide-opens, islets connected by a submarine chain of rounded stones, where St Cuthbert heard the fiends shriek as they played in the spray before storms, and the monks drew a fence of straw signed with the holy cross along the sands between them and a demon pack of goatriders, cowled, black, short and hideous, with long jibing faces.

Gainford

In St Mary's Church on three successive days, according to a saying, the vicar married a pig, christened a lamb, and buried a Hogg.

Galilee Chapel, Durham Cathedral

A large slab of black Frosterley marble in the Galilee Chapel marks the resting place of the Venerable Bede, monk of Monkwearmouth and Jarrow, and author of the *Ecclesiastical History of England*. Bede died at Jarrow and was originally buried in the monastic church of St Paul's. In 1020 the relics of Bede were stolen (probably by order) from the monastic church by a pilgrim and taken to Durham where they were placed in Cuthbert's tomb in a linen bag; afterwards they became inclusions in Cuthbert's magnificent shrine. After the Reformation, Bede's bones were reinterred in the Galilee

The Galilee Chapel, Durham Cathedral, showing the tomb of Bede. (From the *Monthly Chronicle* 'North-Country Lore and Legends', 1890)

Chapel. The story goes that the monk who was originally ordered to compose the epithet for Bede's grave had writer's block. He wrote:

> Hac Sunt in fossa,
> Beda … ossa

But could not find a suitable word to complete the phrase and retired for the night. The next morning to his great surprise that angels had supplied the missing word 'Venerabilis' :

> Hac Sunt in fossa
> Beda Venerabilis ossa

Haughton Castle
Haughton Castle, situated on North Tyne, is haunted by the spectre of an Armstrong mosstrooper.

The owner of Haughton Castle, Sir John de Widdrington, 'a learned and clerkly man' was asked by local landowners to lay a memorial before Cardinal Wolsey, then Bishop of Durham and Archbishop of York as well as Chancellor and Legate a Latere. Before setting out for York (which the cardinal was visiting) the Lord of Haughton's men had captured several mosstroopers including the chief of the Armstrongs, who was brought to Haughton and lodged in the dungeon. Widdrington reached York before he realised that he was carrying the dungeon key. He immediately rode back, but the prisoner was found dead, either from starvation and dehydration or from the foul air. In his mortal agony he had gnawed the flesh from one of his arms and his features were contorted. The spectre of the Armstrong haunted the castle 'in the dead of the night, shrieks of the most agonising kind were heard issuing from the dungeon and resounding through every room in the place'. No servant would stay within its precincts until the rector of Simonburn exorcised the ghost.

Heavenfield
Bede reports that Heavenfield, 'a place pointed out to this day and held in great veneration' was where King Oswald, about to give battle to the Heathen, set up a wooden cross: and that soon after a young man was cured by a portion of it, and thereafter innumerable miracles took place. In Bede's day many folk took splinters of wood from this cross and put them in water, and when any man or beast drank the water 'they were at once restored to health'.

Hell's Hole
Hell's Hole, more commonly called Henhole, is situated on the north side of Great Cheviot where water falls in dramatic cascades. A small cave is set in the face of the highest cliff on the right bank; into this it is said an early Lord Percy along with his hounds, out hunting in the Cheviots, entered and never returned. Another variant of this tale is that hunters heard the sweetest music and were drawn inexplicably in, but could not find their way out again – all except one who 'hesitated' on the brink of the hole and came back to tell the tale. The tale is taken from the *Monthly Chronicle*, 1889.

The site of Oswald's Cross, Heavenfield. (Photo: Geoff Doel)

Hell's Hole, Cheviot Hills. (From the *Monthly Chronicle* – 'North-Country Lore and Legends', late nineteenth century)

Hell's Kettles

Hell's Kettles can be found at Oxen-le-Hall, near Darlington and are supposedly three bottomless pits and foaming with hell's boiling hot green water infested with flesh eating pikes and eels. It is said that geese and ducks thrown in have made their way through passages to the River Tees. An account of 1577 calls them:

> … three little poles, which the people call the Kettles of Hell, or ye Devil's Kettles, as if he should see the souls of sinfull men and women in them; they adde also that ye spirits oft beene harde to cry and yell about them.

Hexham – St Alchmund, 7th Bishop of Hexham, The Fingerless Saint

The relics of the eighth-century St Alchmund were originally buried outside Hexham Abbey, but all trace of his grave was lost during the Danish incursions. The ghost of Alchmund revealed the whereabouts of his bones in around the eleventh century to Alured the sacristan of Durham Cathedral and requested the removal of his remains to a more honourable position in the church. Alured found the bones and quietly removed one of the saint's fingers to carry away to Durham. The saint resented the mutilation. The next day the bearers attempted to remove the coffin, but found the burden too heavy for them. Alchmund again appeared to the dreamer, showed his fingerless hand and demanded his bones should be buried entire, which was done.

Hylton Castle

Hylton Castle stands near turnpike road from Monkwearmouth to Gateshead, for six centuries home of one of the oldest most powerful and best-allied families in Durham. The Hyltons had a fabulous genealogy stretching back to Athelstan and genuine pedigree stretching to Henry II. Legend states that while the Anglo-Saxon lord of Hylton was far away in Eastern lands making love to a Syrian maid his daughter was wooed and won by a Danish knight who first came to her in the guise of a raven. Another famous ghost is the Cauld Lad, whose 'unearthly wailings' were heard around midnight, and after whom a room was named in the castle which was only used 'when the castle was full of company'.

Jarrow

The Venerable Bede (c. 672/3-735) moved from St Peter's Monastery, Monkwearmouth to the linked St Paul's Monastery, Jarrow at or soon after its foundation in 682, and as its Librarian wrote his famous *Ecclesiastical History of the English People*. The monastery was burnt by the Vikings, but re-founded in 1072. In the late Middle Ages a fourteenth-century wooden chair (probably that of an Abbot) was venerated by the pilgrims and this later came to be known as 'Bede's Chair'. Folklore held that a splinter from the chair in water had curative properties. The chair's magical/religious properties are still respected by the local community.

Jingling Geordie's Hole or the Jingler's Hole

This is one of a number of curious caves below Tynemouth Priory and Castle. They were explored in the 1840s and found to consist of two chambers with arched roofs and possible

Bede's Chair – it was commonly believed that women who sit in this chair would soon fall pregnant. (Photo: Geoff Doel)

St Paul's Church, Jarrow, where Bede's chair is kept. (From the *Monthly Chronicle* – 'North-Country Lore and Legends', 1888)

subterranean rooms. Rock falls have prevented further exploration. Variously claimed to be the haunt of fairies, or the hermit cell of Ceolwulf, the eighth-century king of Northumbria to whom the Venerable Bede dedicated his *Ecclesiastical History* and who later became a monk. In later periods it was claimed to be variously inhabited by the Wytche of Tinemouth or alternatively by a sorcerer who was the guardian of a vast store of wealth.

Jock's Leap, Aydon Castle
The owner of the castle, Sir Robert Cleavering, captured a marauding band of Scotsmen and had them thrown one by one to their death down a rocky ravine close to the house in which runs the Cor Burn. Only one of their number survived by making the leap of his life across the gap.

The King's Chair near Wooler
A porphyry crag on the hill above Pin Well.

Lambert's Leap
In Sandyford Lane, Newcastle-upon-Tyne, near the Barras Bridge, can be seen the words 'Lambert's Leap' cut into one of the stones of the bridge. These words commemorate a spectacular near fatality in the mid-eighteenth century. However, later that same century an almost identical accident occurred at exactly the same spot and bizarrely yet another 'copycat' accident occurred fifty years later.

Barras Bridge originally forded a burn which flowed through fields (now disappeared) into Drop Well Ravine and which joined the Ouseburn opposite Heaton Haugh. On 20 September 1759, a young man employed by HM Customs, Cuthbert Lambert, was riding along Sandyford Lane when his mare took fright for no apparent reason and in a blind panic leapt over the parapet of the bridge 'a leap of forty-five feet and thirty-six perpendicular. . Young Lambert managed to keep his seat and the mare broke his fall, though dislocating every bone in her spine and dying almost immediately. Young

Cuthbert was deemed to have had a miraculous escape and news of the spectacular leap brought hundreds of Newcastle sightseers regularly to the bridge, at which point the words Lambert's Leap was cut on one of the coping stones of the bridge.

The incident became a media sensation when in 1786 an engraving of a print recording the accident was made for 'Sporting Anecdotes.' Locals were quick to point out that the original artist had obviously never seen Barras Bridge nor the ravine (nor presumably young Cuthbert).

Only twelve years later a mounted servant of Sir John Hussey of Delaval Hall, Seaton Delaval, made an equally spectacular fall from the parapet of Barras Bridge. This time the man fell beneath his horse and was only saved from being crushed by falling between two large protruding boulders. The rider, as before, escaped with few injuries but the horse was so severely injured it had to be shot.

A third accident took place on 5 December 1827, when a young Newcastle surgeon, John Nicholson, making his way along Sandyford Lane on horseback was unable to stop his horse from leaping down into the Dene over the bridge parapet. This time it was the horse which survived: John Nicholson died that evening from his wounds.

The Legend of the Long Pack

Bellingham, which stands on the very edge of the Northumbrian moors, was once the haunt and target of the marauding 'gaynes' (clans) of the Charltons, Armstrongs, Dodds, Milburns and Robsons. A curious pack-shaped tombstone in St Cuthbert's churchyard is linked with this well-known legend, recounted in the *Monthly Chronicle*. A pedlar called at Lee Hall, the Georgian mansion of Colonel Ridley, an ex-Indian colonial whose house stands by the North Tyne and requested a night's lodging. Because the colonel

St Cuthbert's Church, Bellingham, which is associated with the legend of the Long Pack. (From the *Monthly Chronicle* – 'North-Country Lore and Legends', 1891)

was not at home, the maid, Alice, refused but allowed the man to leave his heavy pack in the kitchen. Later in the evening she noticed that the pack was moving, and sought help. A ploughboy fired a bullet into the pack, whereupon blood poured out. Inside was found the body of a young man with a silver horn. The servants realised that this was a Trojan Horse situation, mustered help, and when they were ready blew the silver horn. The unsuspecting robbers arrived but they were met with more than they had bargained for and fled. The unknown man in the pack was buried in Bellingham churchyard.

Muggleswick Churchyard
The churchyard contains the grave of seventeenth-century giant John Ward, so large that a 'favourite hound of his littered in his wooden shoe'.

Neville's Cross
The tradition is that Lord Neville erected at his own cost a magnificent cross on the spot where the corporax or chalice cover affixed to a spear had served as the standard for the English forces in the Battle of Neville's Cross against the Scots on 17 October 1346. The monks of Durham had extemporised a standard by fastening to a spear handle the holy cloth connected with St Cuthbert, who appeared in a dream the night before battle to King David of Scotland, warning him to spare the sacred treasures of Durham. David II had 30,000 men plus a contingent from the French King and the especially holy Black Rood of the House of Bruce studded with gems. The English were victorious and King David was captured and ransomed the following year for 100,000 marks.

The Norham Cross
The Norham Cross, described as 'a queer pyramidical cross', stands in the centre of the green at Norham. Traditionally it is said to be the site where the Irish missionaries from Iona first preached Christianity.

Raby Castle
Robert Surtees wrote to Cuthbert Sharp that the first Lord Barnard and his wife disliked their son and decided to pull down the castle and he stopped them by an injunction in Chancery. Surtees recounts the supernatural tale that resulted:

> This old jade after her death used to drive about in the air, in a black coach and six; sometimes she takes the ground and drives slowly up the town to Alice's Well, and still more frequently walks the battlements of Raby, with a pair of brass knitting needles, and is called the Old Hell Cat. Why she carries brass knitting needles, and why she hated her son so, is unexplained.

St Nicholas' Church Steeple, Newcastle-upon-Tyne
One of the most cherished legends, recounted in the *Monthly Chronicle*, ascribes the preservation of St Nicholas' Church during the siege by the Scots in 1644:

> In the time of the Civil Wars when the Scots had besieged the town for several weeks, General [Lesley] sent a Messenger to the Mayor of the Town, [Marley], and demanded the Keys, and the Delivering up of the Town, or he would immediately demolish the Steeple of

Norham Castle. (Photo: Geoff Doel)

St Nicholas'. The Mayor and Alderman upon hearing this, immediately ordered a certain Number of the chiefest of the Scottish Prisoners to be carried up to the Top of the old Tower, the Place below the Lanthorne, and there confined; after this they returned the general an Answer to this Purpose, That they would upon no Terms deliver up the Town, but would to the last Moment defend it; that the Steeple of St Nicholas was indeed a beautiful and magnificent piece of Architecture, and one of the great ornaments of their Town; but yet should be blown into Attoms before ransom'd at such a Rate: That, however, it was to fall, it should not fall alone; that the same Moment he destroyed the beautiful Structure Bath his Hands in the Blood of his Countrymen; who were placed there on Purpose either to preserve it from Ruin, or to die along with it. This Message had the desired Effect. The Men were there kept prisoners during the whole Time of the Siege, and no so much as one Gun fired against it.

Shaftoe Crags
Shaftoe Crags, within walking distance of Bolam, has a 'remarkable punch-bowl hollowed out of the flat sandstone rock. Legend describes the Romans making celebratory drinks in it'.

Wardon Law
Wardon Law is the highest hill on Eastern coast of Durham and is situated midway between Seaham harbour and Houghton-le-Spring. Traditionally it is believed to be where the bones of St Cuthbert rested before they were interred at Durham.

'Winter's Stob', Elsdon
Winter's Stob is the name of a gibbet still standing on a hill south-east of Elsdon, an isolated and atmospheric moorland village near the Scottish border. The *Monthly Chronicle* tells the following tale:

Steng Cross Gallows, also known as Winter's Stob, near Elsdon. (Photo: Geoff Doel)

In earlier times Elsdon was the gathering place for the Redesdale clan and performed the ritual of driving cattle through the midsummer bonfire. In August 1791 an elderly woman called Margaret Crozier who lived in an old Peel House at a place called the Raw near Elsdon and ran a small drapery was found dead in her bed; her throat had been cut and one hand lacerated. The murder occasioned great excitement and a reward of five pounds was offered to be 'paid on conviction of the offender or offenders'. Suspicion fell on three strangers who had been noted in the vicinity, a man, William Winter, and two women. All were connected with what are called in Northumberland 'Faw' gangs – clans of gipsies living in the Borders (The Scots called them 'Faas'). They were imprisoned in Morpeth goal (William in solitary confinement) for 11 months until their trial in the Moot Hall, Newcastle. All three were found guilty and sentenced to be hanged at outside Westgate where a gallows was erected. The bodies of the women were given to surgeons to be dissected but William's body was destined to be gibbeted at Steng cross, within sight of the Raw, in the clothes he had worn when executed. Straps of iron bound his limbs and chest and the head enclosed in iron bands. The shaft was thirty foot high and driven full of large headed spike nails. As the body decayed what remained were hung in a new sack, tarred inside and out. As this also decayed materials passing shepherds cleared away and buried. Thousands of visitors on foot and horseback. The place became a place of pilgrimage for the 'Faw' gangs. In 1889 the stob had been removed, there were no nails in the upright post and a wooden head had been made which hung from the cross beams.

The Woods of Ladykirk, Norham

James IV of Scotland set up the chapel in 'gratitude for having been preserved from drowning in a dangerous passage of the Tweed'.

NOTES

When referring to books, just the author's surname will be given, further details being found in the bibliography.

Introduction
For a fine historical, cultural and religious survey see Hunter Blair.
For discussions of Bede's *De Temporum Ratione* and the heathen year see Owen and Hutton.

Chapter One
For the Laidley worm see Child and Kinloch, plus engagement with Simpson's and Westwood's alternative theories. Ballad text from Child given as Appendix 1.
For the Lambton Worm see *Denham Tracts*, Cuthbert Sharpe, Newman; text of song by C.M. Numans in Appendix 2.

Chapter Two
For Fawdon Hill see the *Monthly Chronicle*, 1891, 28.
For Staindrop's version of the Talking Cat see the *Monthly Chronicle*, 1889.
For legends of the Kow see the *Monthly Chronicle*, 1889.
For the Picktree Brag see the *Monthly Chronicle*, 1891.
An account of the Brown Man is given in Surtees in his *History of Durham* iv.
For colliery superstitions and beliefs in the nineteenth century see the *Colliery Guardian*, 23 May 1863.

Chapter Three
For an account of Netherwitton Fairies see Brockie.
For 'Aad Wilson' see the *Monthly Chronicle*, 1891.
For an account of Lady Jarratt see Longstaffe and Brockie.
For Hob Hedeless see Longstaffe and Brockie.
For the Hylton Brag see Brockie.
Sedgefield's Pickled Parson – an account by Brockie and WB is in the *Monthly Chronicle*, 1891 also 1887.
For silkies, white ladies etc see Denham, Richardson and the *Monthly Chronicle*, 1887.
For silky-type legends from South Shields which resemble those of Lady Jarrett see Brockie's the *Northern Tribune*, 1855, also quoted in the *Monthly Chronicle*, 1888.

For the Pelton Brag see Cuthbert Sharp's *Bishoprick Garland* (1834).
For an account of ghostly armies at Neville's Cross see Brockie.
For traditions regarding Peg Powler see Longstaffe and Denham.

Chapter Four
For the Arthurian Sewingshields legends see Hodgson and Ashe.
For Joyeus Gard see Malory.
For Derwentwater see Surtees.

Chapter Five
For Dorothy Forster see Bird, Besant and Forster.
For Betty Surtees see the *Monthly Chronicle*, 1888 and the *Monthly Chronicle* 1890.
For Miss Bell see the *Monthly Chronicle*, 1891.
Sources for Grace Darling include material from the Grace Darling Museum, Bamburgh,
    Darling and Hope, and Algernon Swinburne's poem 'Grace Darling'.

Chapter Six
For the life of Cuthbert see Bede.
For the tale of Cuthbert and the Pictish princess see the *Monthly Chronicle*, 1988.
For Cuthbert as misogynist see Schulenburg.
For Cuthbert's miracles see Finucane, Webb and Sumption.
Cuthbert's Community is dealt with in Bonner.

Chapter Seven
For details of Godric and Bartholomew see Tudor's article in *Farmer*.
For details of the Gateshead anchorite see the *Monthly Chronicle*, 1887.
For hermits and anchorites in the north see Clay.

Chapter Eight
For details of the Jesmond well see Brewis. For holy wells in Northumberland and Durham
    see Binnall.

Chapter Nine
For a full transcript of the Examination of Elizabeth Simpson of Tynemouth, see Surtees
    Society, vol. 40.
For the Confession of Alice Swan see *Ecclesiastical Proceedings*, Surtees Society, vol. 20 (1854).
For the Bishop of Durham proceeding against Katherine Thompson and Anne Nevelson see
    the *Visitation Book*, Registration Office, Durham and Richardson's *Table Book I*.
The story of the magician Michael Scott appears in *Denham Tracts II*.
For the Easington Witch see Brockie.

Chapter Ten
For food see *Denham Tracts*.
For Christmas and New Year Traditions see *Denham Tracts* and Balfour.
For divination see *Denham Tracts*.
For Allendale Bonfire see Day.
For mummers plays see *Denham Tracts*.
For sword dancers see Brand, Balfour, Cuthbert Sharp, Cecil Sharp and FARNE (Folk Archive
    Research North East).
For Shrovetide customs see Aperley and the *Monthly Chronicle*.

For Easter see Balfour and Hutchinson.
For May customs see Brand, Hutchinson and Mackenzie.
For midsummer bonfires see Stone.
For harvest see Denham and Stone.
For Riding the Stang see the *Monthly Chronicle* & Denham.
For Gaudy Days see Denham.
For Hallowe'en see *History of Alnwick* (1813).

Chapter Eleven

See Apperley, Denham, Brand, Surtees, Cockburn, Ridley, Egglestone, and the *Monthly Chronicle*, 1887 & 1890.
For traditions regarding the stob see Murray.

Chapter Twelve

See Rutherford, *Northumbrian Minstrelsy* and collections by Percy, Ritson, Bell, Denham, Shields, Telfer and Lloyd.

Chapter Thirteen

In this gazetteer the sources are cited for most of the entries, prominent among which are the *Monthly Chronicle*, the *Denham Tracts* and Robert Surtees. Simpson and Westwood's *Lore of the Land* is an excellent recent book with helpful chapters on the legendary landscape of Durham and Northumberland. Oral information on the Great Storm and Berwick was from James Petrie, and James Guy, churchwarden of St Paul's, Jarrow, provided information on Bede's Chair.

THE BALLAD OF 'THE LAIDLEY WORM OF SPINDLESTON HEUGHS'

The king is gone from Bambrough castle,
Long may the princess mourn;
Long may she stand on the castle wall,
Looking for his return.

She has knotted the keys upon a string,
And with her she has them taen,
She has cast them oer hr left shoulder,
And to the gate she is gane.

She tripped out, she tripped in,
She tript into the yard;
But it was more for the king's sake,
Than for the queen's regard.

It fell out on a day the king
Bought the queen with him home,
And all the lords in our country
To welcome them did come.

'O welcome, father,' the lady cries,
'Unto your halls and bowers;
And so are you, my stepmother,
For all that is here is yours.'

A lord said, wondering while she spake,
This princess of the North
Surpasses all of female kind
In beauty and in worth.

The envious queen replied: 'At least,
You might have excepted me;
In a few hours I will hr bring
Down to a low degree.'

'I will her liken to a laidley worm,
That warps about the stone,
And not till Childy Wynd comes back
Shall she again be won.'

The princess stood at the bower door,
Laughing, who could her blame?
But eer the next day's sun went down,
A long worm she became.

For seven miles east, and seven miles west,
And seven miles north and south,
No blade of grass or corn could grow,
So venomous was her mouth.

The milk of seven stately cows –
It was costly her to keep –
Was brought her daily, which she drank
Before she went to sleep.

At this day may be seen the cave
Which held her folded up,
And the stone trough, the very same
Out of which she did sup.

Word went east, and word went west,
And word is gone over the sea,
That a laidley worm in Spindleston Heughs
Would ruin the north country.

Word went east, and word went west,
And over the sea did go;
The Child of Wynd got wit of it,
Which filled his heart with woe.

He called straight his merry men all,
They thirty were and three:
'I wish I were at Spindleston,
This desperate worm to see.

'We have no time now here to waste,
Hence quickly let us sail;
My only sister Margaret,
Something, I fear, doth ail.'

They built a ship without delay,
With masts of the rowan tree,
With fluttering sails of silk so fine,
And set her on the sea.

They went aboard; the wind with speed
Blew them along the deep;
At length they spied an huge square tower,
On a rock high and steep.

The sea was smooth, the weather clear;
When they approached nigher,
King Ida's castle they well knew,
And the banks of Bambroughshire.

The queen looked out at her bower-window,
To see what she could see;
There she espied a gallant ship,
Sailing upon the sea.

When she beheld the silken sails,
Full glancing in the sun,
To sink the ship she sent away
Her witch-wives every one.

Their spells were vain; the hags returned
To the queen in sorrowful mood,
Crying that witches have no power
Where there is rowan-tree wood.

Her last effort, she sent a boat,
Which in the haven lay
With armed men to board the ship,
But they were driven away.

The worm leapt up, the worm leapt down,
She plaited round the stane;
And ay as the ship came to the land
She banged it off again.

The Child then ran out of her reach
The ship on Budle sand,
And jumping into the shallow sea,
Securely got to land.

And now he drew his berry-brown sword,
And laid it on her head,
And swore, if she did harm to him,
That he would strike her dead.

'O quit thy sword, and bend thy bow,
And give me kisses three;
For though I am a poisonous worm,
No hurt I will do to thee.'

'O quit thy sword, and bend thy bow,
And give me kisses three;
If I am not won eer the sun go down,
Won I shall never be.'

He quitted his sword, he bent his brow,
He gave her kisses three;
She crept into a hole a worm,
But stepped out a lady.

No clothing had this lady fine,
To keep her from the cold;
He took his mantle from him about,
And round her did it fold.

He has taken his mantle from him about,
And it he wrapt her in,
And they are up to Bambrough castle,
As fast as they can win.

His absence and her serpent shape
The king had long deplored;
He now rejoiced to see them both
Again to him restored.

The queen they wanted, whom they found
All pale, and sore afraid,
Because she knew her power must yield
To Childy Wynd's, who said:

'Woe be to thee, thou wicked witch,
An ill death mayest thou dee;
As thou my sister hast likened,
So likened shalt thou be.

'I will turn you into a toad,
That on the ground doth wend,
And won, won shalt thou never be,
Till this world hath an end.'

Now on the sand near Ida's tower,
She crawls a loathsome toad,
And venom spits on every maid
She meets upon her road.

The virgins all of Bambrough town
Will swear that they have seen
This spiteful toad, of monstrous size,
Whilst walking they have been.

All folks believe within the shire
This story to be true,
And they all run to Spindleston,
The cave and trough to view.

This fact now Duncan Frasier,
Of Cheviot, sings in rhime,
Lest Bambroughshire men should forget
Some part of it in time.

From Francis Child's *The English & Scottish Ballads*, vol. 1, pp. 311-3. In turn taken from William Hutchinson's *A View of Newcastle* (1778) to which it was supplied by Revd Lamb of Norham, who probably wrote most of it himself (though attributing it to Duncan Frasier), although Child considers there are fragments of an original ballad in it.

'THE LAMBTON WORM'
BY C.M. LEUMANS (1867)

One Sunday mornin' Lambton went a fishin' in the Wear;
An' catched a fish up on he's heuk he thowt leuk't vary queer
But whatt'n a kind ov fish it was young Lambon cuddent tell
He waddn't fash te carry'd hyem, so he hoyed it in a well.

Chorus
Whisht! lads, haad yor gobs, an' aa'll tell ye aall an aaful story,
Whisht! lads, haad yor gobs, an' aa'll tell ye 'boot the worm.

Noo Lambton felt inclined te gan an' fight I' foreign wars.
He joined a troop ov Knights that caed for nowther woonds nor scars,
An' 'off he went te Palestine whee queer things him befell,
An vay seum forgat aboot the queer worm I' the well.

But the worm got fat an' growed an' growed, an' growed an aaful size;
He'd greet big teeth, a greet big gob, an' greet big goggle eyes.
An' when at neets he craaled aboot te pick up bits o' news,
If he feld dry upon the road, he milked a dozen coos.

This fearful worm would often feed on caalves an' lambs an' sheep,
An' swally little bairns alive when they laid doon te sleep.
An' when he'd eaten aall he cud an' he had had he's fill,
He craaled away an' lapped he's tail ten times roond Pensher Hill.

The news ov this myest aaful worm an' his queer gannins on
Seun crossed the seas, gat te the ears ov brave an' bowld Sor John,
So hyem he cam an' catched the beast an cut 'im in twe halves,
An' that seun stopped hes eatin' bairns an' sheep an' lambs an' calves.

So noo ye knaa hoo aall the foaks on byeth sides ov the Wear
Lost lots o' shep an' lots o'sleep an' leeved i' mortal feor.
So let's hev one te brave Sor John that kept the bairns frae harm,
Saves coos an' calves by myekin' halves o' the famis Lambton Worm.

Final Chorus
Noo, lads, a'll haad me gob, that's aall aa knaa aboot the story
Ov Sor John's clivvor job wi' the aaful Lambton Worm.

SELECT BIBLIOGRAPHY

BOOKS

Anon *The History of Alnwick, the County Town of Northumberland* (Alnwick, 1813)

Anon *History of Berwickshire Naturalists' Club* 16 vols (Edinburgh, 1833–1899)

Apperley, Newton 'Folk-Lore of the County of Durham' in *Memorials of Old Durham* (London, 1910)

Ashe, Geoffrey *A Guidebook to Arthurian Britain* (Longman: London, 1980)

Balfour, M.C., & Thomas, N.W. *County Folklore: vol. IV: Northumberland* (Folklore Society: London, 1904)

Bede *Ecclesiastical History of the English People* (Penguin: London, 1990)

Bell, John *Rhymes of Northern Bards, Being a Curious Collection of Old and New Songs and Poems Peculiar to the Counties of Newcastle upon Tyne, Northumberland and Durham* (1812)

Bird, John *Dorothy and the Forsters of Bamburgh* (John Bird, 1982)

Bonner, Gerald, Rollason, David & Stancliffe, Clare (eds) *St Cuthbert, His Cult & His Community to A.D. 1200* (Woodbridge: The Boydell Press, 1989)

Bourne, Henry *Antiquitates Vulgares* (Newcastle-upon-Tyne, 1727)

Brand, John *History & Antiquities of the Town and County of Newcastle-upon-Tyne* (Newcastle-upon-Tyne, London, 1839)

Brand, John *Observations on the Popular Antiquities of Great Britain*, ed. Sir Henry Ellis

Binnall P.B.G. 'Holy Wells in Northumberland and Durham', *Proceedings of the Society of Antiquaries of Newcastle-upon-Tyne*, 4th series, vol. IX, no. 10 (1942)

Bird, John *Dorothy and the Forster of Bamburgh* (How & Blackhall: Berwick-upon-Tweed, 1982)

Brewis P. 'St. Mary's Chapel and the Site of St Mary's Well, Jesmond,' *Archaeologia Aeliana,* 4th series, vol. 5 (1928)

Brockie, William *Legends & Superstitions of the County of Durham* (Sunderland, 1886)

Child, Francis James *The English & Scottish Popular Ballads* (Little Brown: Boston, 1882–98; reprint, New York: Dover, 1965)

Clay, Rotha Mary *The Hermits and Anchorites of England* (Methuen, 1913)

Cockburn, Florence N. 'The Legends of Durham' in *Memorials of Old Durham* (London, 1910)

Collingwood Buce, J. & Stokoe, John *Northumbrian Minstrelsy* (Society of Antiquities: Newcastle-upon-Tyne, 1882)

Dark, Ken *Britain and the End of the Roman Empire* (Tempus: Stroud, 2000)

Darling, Thomasin *Grace Darling, her True Story: from Unpublished Papers in possession of her Family* (1880)

Darling, Thomasin *The Journal of William Darling, Grace Darling's Father* (1887)

Day, Brian *A Chronicle of Folk Customs* (Hamlyn: London, 1998)

Denham, Michael *Denham Tracts*, 2 vols, ed. Hardy, James (Folklore Society: London, 1892–5)

Dixon, James Henry *Ancient Poems, Ballads and Songs of the Peasantry of England* (1846)

Douglas, Marion *Tales and Legends in Northumbria* (1934)

Egglestone, W.M. 'Charms for Venom' in *North Country Lore and Legend* (1889)

Ewen, C. L'Estrange *Witch Hunting and Witch Trials* (London, 1929)

Farmer, David *The Oxford Dictionary of Saints* (OUP: Oxford, 1982)

Finucane, Ronald C. *Miracles and Pilgrims, Popular Beliefs in Medieval England* (Dent & Sons Ltd, 1977)

Grice, F. *Folk Tales of the North Country* (Thomas Nelson & Sons Ltd, 1944)

Harrison, Helena, 'The Folk-Lore of Cumberland, Northumberland & Durham' in *Three Counties of England* ed. Headlam, Cuthbert

Headlam Cuthbert (ed) *Three Northern Counties of England* (Northumberland Press Ltd: Gateshead, 1939)

Henderson, William *Notes on the Folk-Lore of the Northern Counties of England & the Borders* (Longmans Green: London, 1866; reprint, EP: Wakefield, 1973)

Hodgson, John *History of Northumberland* (Newcastle-upon-Tyne, 1827–1840)

Hope, Eva *Grace Darling – Heroine of the Farne Islands* (Walter Scott, 1880)

Hunter Blair, Peter *Northumbria in the Days of Bede* (Llanerch: Felinfach, 1976, reprint 1996)

Hutchinson, William *The History & Antiquities of the County Palatine of Durham*, 3 vols (Newcastle-upon-Tyne, 1785)

Hutchinson, William *View of Northumberland*, 3 vols (Newcastle-upon-Tyne, 1778)

Hutton, Ronald *Stations of the Sun* (OUP: Oxford, 1996)

Kinloch, George Ritchie *Papers for Ancient Scottish Ballads Recovered from Tradition and Never Before Published*, vol. 1 (1827)

Leighton, Henry R. *Memorials of Old Durham* (London, 1910)

Longstaffe, W. Hylton Dyer *History of the parish of Darlington* (1854)

Lloyd, A.L. *Come All Ye Bold Miners* (Lawrence & Wishart: London, 1952, revised 1978)

Mackenzie, E. *An Historical, Topographical, and Descriptive View of the County of Northumberland*, 2 vols. (Newcastle-upon-Tyne, 1825)

Malory, Sir Thomas *Le Morte D'Arthur* (OUP: Oxford, 1998)

Murray *Handbook for Northumberland and Durham* (London, 1864)

Newman, Paul *The Hill of the Dragon* (Rowman & Littlefield: Totowa N.J., 1980)

Notes and Queries (London, 1849, etc)

Oliver, Stephen (W.A. Chatto) *Rambles in Northumberland* (London, 1835)

Owen, Gale *Rites and Religions of the Anglo-Saxons* (David & Charles: Newton Abbot, 1981)

Peacock, John *Favourite Collection of Tunes with Variations Adapted for the Northumbrian Small Pipes, Violin or Flute* (c. 1820)

Percy, Thomas *Reliques of Ancient English Poetry* (Swan Sonnenschein & Co: London, 1765, reprint 1910)

Raine, James *The History and Antiquities of North Durham. By the Revd James Raine* (London, 1852)

Richardson, M.A. *The Local Historian's Table Book of Remarkable Occurrences in two parts* historical, 5 vols, legendary, 2 vols (Newcastle-upon-Tyne, 1838-1846) re-issued as the Borderer's Table Book. (London, 1846)

Ridley, Nancy *Northumberland Then and Now* (London, 1978)

Rutherford, Frank 'The Collecting and Publishing of Northumbrian Folk-Song' *Archaeologia Aeliana* 4 XLII

Schulenburg, Jane Tibbetts *Forgetful of Their Sex* (Chicago University Press: Chicago, 1998)

Sharp, Cecil *The Sword Dances of Northern England* (Novello: London, 1911–13)

Sharpe, Cuthbert *Bishoprick Garland* (London, 1834)

Simpson, Jacqueline & Westwood, Jennifer *The Lore of the Land* (Penguin: London, 2005)

Stokoe, John *Songs and Ballads of Northern England* (1893)

Stone, Sir Benjamin *Sir Benjamin Stone's Pictures: Records of National Life & History, vol. 1 Festivals, Ceremonies & Customs* (Cassell: London, 1906)

Sumption Jonathan *Pilgrimage* (Faber & Faber: London, 1975)

Surtees, Robert *The History & Antiquities of the County Palatine of Durham* (Durham, 1816-40)

The Publications of the Surtees Society, vol. 40 *Depositions from the Castle of York relating to Offences committed in the Northern Counties in the Seventeenth Century,* Edited by J. Raine. (Newcastle-upon-Tyne, 1861)

Surtees Society *The Rites of Durham* Publications of the Surtees Society, vol. 107 (1593)

Terry, Jean F. *Northumberland Yesterday and To-day* (Andre Reid & Co.: Newcastle-upon-Tyne, 1913)

Tomlinson, W.W. *Life in Northumberland During the Sixteenth Century* (Walter Scott Ltd: London)

Topliff, Robert *Melodies of the Tyne and the Wear*

Tudor V.M. 'St Godric and St Bartholomew' in Farmer, D.H. (ed) *Benedict's Disciples* (1995)

Scott, Walter *Monthly Chronicle of North-Country Lore and Customs* (Newcastle-upon-Tyne 1887, 1889, 1890)

Webb Diana *Pilgrims and Pilgrimage* (Tauris: New York, 2001)

Whittaker, W.G. *North Countrie Ballads, Songs and Pipe-Tunes, for Use in Home and School* (1921)

PERIODICALS

Archaologia Aeliana, Transactions of the Society of Antiquaries of Newcastle 4 vols (1822–1825) new series, 24 vols (1857–1903)

Monthly Chronicle of North Country Lore and Legend, vols 1–5 (Newcastle-upon-Tyne, 1887–91)

Proceedings of the Society of Antiquaries of Newcastle-upon-Tyne, N.S. Vols 1–10 (Newcastle-upon-Tyne, 1882–1902)

WEBSITES

Folk Archive Research North East (FARNE)

INDEX